"Jeffrey has
beyond his years and skillfully puts into words the truths that
every parent should know."

> *- Fern O'Shea, 50 yr. old mother and grandmother.*

"Parents! Read this book and increase the depth, meaning and
vision for your greatest task; raising an excellent generation."

> *- Todd Brown, 35 yr. old father of three.*

"Each of the stories and analogies in this book taught powerful
lessons. Fair Warning provides a compelling perspective that every
parent must experience and seriously consider."

> *- Lori Campbell, 34 year old mother of three and Founder,*
> *How To Be a Mother, Inc.*

"My greatest ambition is to someday know the joys of being a
successful parent. I find this book to be a breath of fresh air as it .
addresses the many concerns I have about raising children in
today's world. Jeff Chavez presents insights deeply rooted in prin-
ciple and truth that will aid any person trying to be the best pos-
sible parent. Fair Warning is an undeniable reminder of the
information about life that every child deserves to receive!"

> *- Scott Ditty, teacher, 34 years old.*

"This book motivated my wife and I to become a little better
ourselves and to make more specific and careful plans for raising
our two girls to succeed, not just get by. It was one of the best
books I have ever read."

> *- Brandon Clark, 26 yr. old father of two.*

QUICK
SILVER
PRESS

FAIR

WARNING

Making Good
Children Great
and
Turning Ordinary Parents Into
American Heroes

A PERSPECTIVE ON PARENTING FROM
GENERATION X

Jeffrey A. Chavez

QUICK
SILVER

PRESS

Quicksilver Communications
26741 Portola Pkwy
Suite 1E-222
Foothill Ranch, CA 92610

The actual names of most individuals included in
this book have been changed.

Published by Quicksilver Press,
a subsidiary of Quicksilver Communications

First Edition, 1998

Book Design and Cover by Paul Jager
SEEING EYE STUDIOS, Inc.

Edited by Jane Baker

Manufactured in the United States of America
10 9 8 7 6 5 4 3 2

Library of Congress Catalog Card Number: 97-92544

ISBN 0-9659394-0-5
0-9659394-1-3 Pbk.

Dedicated to my entire family

Acknowledgments

I express sincere thanks and appreciation for my wife Shana, who has allowed me to take many risks and has encouraged me to go after my dreams. She exhibits unusual patience and compassion as she raises our girls, Allison and Darcy. I am humbled to be her partner.

This book would not have been possible without the help and support of two of my best and closest friends, Mom and Dad. Their friendship and *Fair Warnings* about life helped me understand what is most important.

I cannot express enough how grateful I am for two big brothers, Chris and Greg, who are consistent examples to me and who, at different times, literally saved my life.

As for the production of and contributions to this book, I extend my sincere thanks to:

- Shana for providing a workable environment in a child-ruled home. And for her invaluable opinions, corrections, and suggestions for this book.

- My father, Larry, for his approval, encouragement and confidence, which significantly enhance my performance in all I set out to accomplish. And for his wisdom and invaluable proofreading and editing abilities. He has an incredible mind.

- My mother, Karen, who has my deepest respect and whose constant praise and encouragement helped me move forward with this endeavor.

- My brothers for allowing me to share some personal experiences, which are included in this book and for providing their thoughts on the project.

- My mother-in-law, Nanci Woodroof, for her feedback and perspective on the beginning drafts.

- Alan Short and Mike Ward who provided important perspective and editing skills.

- Conni Chavez, Rozeanne Chavez, Scott Ditty, Jim Carter, Lisa Mack, Fern O'Shea, Todd Brown, Eric and Julie Lundquist, Lori Campbell, Brandon Clark, Lee Benson, Tiffany Leon, Jack and JoAnne Rushton, Mark Victor Hansen and Peter Vidmar were all kind enough to read and comment on portions of the book in its early stages.

- Jane Baker for her counsel and editing expertise.

- Paul Jager for his exceptional creativity and design contributions.

- My many family members, friends, companions and associates all of whom cannot all be named here and to a few friends who have particularly impacted my life for good: David Maddux, Garth and Edna Lou Eames, Larry and Kathy Call, Ken and Barbi Spangler, and John Campbell.

CONTENTS

Children Learn What They Live

If a child lives with criticism, he learns to condemn.

If a child lives with hostility, he learns to fight.

If a child lives with fear, he learns to be apprehensive.

If a child lives with pity, he learns to feel sorry for himself.

If a child lives with jealousy, he learns to hate.

If a child lives with encouragement, he learns to be confident.

If a child lives with tolerance, he learns to be patient.

If a child lives with praise, he learns to be appreciative.

If a child lives with acceptance, he learns to love.

If a child lives with approval, he learns to like himself.

If a child lives with recognition, he learns to have a goal.

If a child lives with fairness, he learns justice.

If a child lives with security, he learns to have faith in himself and those around him.

If a child lives with honesty, he learns what truth is.

If a child lives with friendliness, he learns that the world is a nice place in which to live.

- Dorthy L. Nolte

Preface

I come to you as one who has recently emerged from the vital teen years. I'm a Generation Xer (born between 1961-1981) who has survived. I know what it is like to grow up as a teen in the 80s and 90s; and there is virtually nothing reported about today's teens today that I have not been in some way personally involved with or effected by.

I believe my life literally hung in the balance as a teen toward eventual success or toward a lifetime of failures and difficulties. Opportunities to do wrong influenced and seemed to engulf me on a regular basis. I was confronted with sneaking into Tim Morgan's alcohol cabinet while his parents were away for the weekend when I was in the 4th grade. During the summer of that same year my friend, Jimmy Taylor, showed me his dad's two-and-a-half foot stack of pornographic magazines, which sat in the living room bookcase. In the 6th grade my grandmother's 14 year-old neighbor invited me to his bedroom to watch him smoke marijuana while his parents watched The Joker's Wild in the next room. Between 7th and 9th grade I was offered cocaine, ecstasy, and LSD. Then I watched as one of my closest friends strung himself out on cocaine and dropped out of school for a year and a half. By the time I was 16 years old, nearly all of my male friends, except for myself and a few others, had lost their virginity. I was aware of acts of cheating, theft, and vandalism among school associates as early as elementary school and saw these activities greatly proliferate as I went through my high school years. I watched violent gang fights at our campus on a monthly basis. During my senior year, a member of my wrestling team was shot and killed in a drive-by shooting. One of the first girls I ever had a crush on, committed suicide the night of our senior prom.

All of these things took place in a nice, suburban community in Southern California. I shudder to think of the stories of temptation and negative persuasion inner city youth can tell.

Now in 1997 at 26 years old, I am happily married to a fantastic woman and the father of two beautiful daughters, Allison and Darcy. I am the sole proprietor of a successful business and own a modest home in a suburban area of Southern California. I come from a middle income household where both Mom and Dad worked year after year rearing three boys. I am thoroughly optimistic about life and look forward to creating a future of happiness for my own family and those around me no matter what hand we are dealt over the coming years.

Thankfully, my life has both purpose and direction. Thankfully, as a teen I made the decision to walk away from the pitfalls of society that so many in my generation and in every generation for that matter, fall into and find themselves trapped in.

Why? Why do I possess this optimism and direction in my life? Why did I escape the trappings when so many others did not? Why was I able to recognize my mistakes and make a change when others did not? Why do so many of my then friends and associates from my teenage years, along with so many others, fit the negative *Generation X* stereotype today? These people are without any real direction, uncertain, and ever-entangled in problems, living for the now and lacking confidence for the future. Why do more and more youth follow in the misguided footsteps of these cool Generation X types than in the footsteps of those who have chosen the paths to success and productivity? Why do so many pass up the opportunity to begin early adulthood with the tremendous advantages resulting from a foundation based on good decisions made as teenagers? What makes the difference?

The difference is in the home. There is a direct and undeniable correlation between what is taught in the home and the strength and ability of young people to begin making the choices in life that will lead them to either inevitable sorrow or unparalleled joy. Many youth fall into the traps of sex, drugs, violence, racism, and laziness, simply because they are largely left to their own devices, lacking knowledge, void of wisdom, and without consistent direction and loving guidance from parents. In many cases, these experiences may prove to haunt their lives for many years, even a lifetime.

Somewhere between my 19th and 21st year, I realized that I was finally becoming a man. This realization occurred not because I knew very much about life. I didn't and still have much to learn. It was due to the fact that during those formative years, I took what I had learned from my parents and from my previous trials and errors and I resolved that I would live the best life I knew how. I resolved that I would make whatever sacrifices were necessary to do so. I began to recognize the long-term value of some vital decisions I had made as a teen. Decisions such as turning my back on drugs and other common indulgences. I began to see that some of my long-time associates were on a road of difficulty due to the careless decisions many of them had made during their formative years. I began to comprehend more completely the things I had been taught in my home pertaining to work, responsibility, character and virtue.

I now began to recognize the wisdom in the multitude of *Warning* signs which my parents placed before me. I began to recognize the *Heroism* of my parents, which I had not understood or recognized earlier. I crossed the bridge linking my parents' rules and guidelines to my own personal rules and guidelines. I was beginning to find congruence with the wisdom of my parents.

This occurred as I began to face the realities of life. I knew I needed and wanted to make good decisions pertaining to the direction of my life and my future. Where would I go? What would I do? Should I get married? How would I support a family? How would I achieve my goals? I found these questions and the answers to them were far more significant to my life compared to the years of trivial teen decisions about what to wear and how to break up with her...on the phone or in person.

Now I could see I had serious decisions to make concerning my life. Now I could see that life is a continual process of correcting our mistakes and gradually improving ourselves. Thankfully, I now lived by these principles for myself having fully recognized the need for such personal guidelines. I now owned the teachings of my parents, learned at a very early age.

There are countless, unheralded *Generation Xers* and other individuals who have made that same resolve. And despite the unending, day-to-day difficulties of life they are achieving great things and are living wonderful lives. But there are many more who simply have not. They have not yet claimed their roles as true men or women but continue to linger in the now and squander their potential on the lesser, temporary pleasures of life. Only later do they find themselves in a state of disappointment and difficulty when they do not receive the lasting gratification they expected.

Many of these teen-minded individuals are not just *Generation Xers* Many of them are 40, 50, and 60 years old. Some of them are drug addicts on the street. Some of them are executives in major corporations. Some are your average, unassuming neighbors who exhibit the lack of true manhood or womanhood each day by deferring their opportunity to create strong children. They do this by allowing the media, schools and peers to shape their children's lives and become their most significant influence. These people are simultaneously unaware or simply not concerned that their greatest opportunities for real joy and satisfaction in life are swiftly passing them by.

With such truths in mind, I became determined to deliver an important and unique message. A message which would hit home and affect a wide range of parents and future parents. I spent over two years researching and compiling valuable information on the family. I reviewed, outlined, and organized the important lessons I learned from my parents as well as through my own experiences. I pondered the perspectives and backgrounds of the many youth that I have had the opportunity to teach about living lives of principle. I present over 150 such classes to teens each year. These experiences and my thoughts pertaining to them were originally recorded on over 1000 pages of journal entries throughout my childhood and young adult years. *Fair Warning* is the result of this effort.

Introduction

FAIR WARNING: A commitment by parents to carefully teach and forewarn their children about the many short- and long-term dangers of life. Such dangers include drugs, violence, sex, negative attitudes, running with the wrong crowd and unkindness. FAIR WARNING also refers to a dedication by parents to instill in their children the virtues of honesty, hard work, humility, self discipline and service to others.

I recall the story of Roy Reigels, who after recovering a fumble in the 1929 Rose Bowl and in a state of disorientation, ran the length of the field toward the end zone. He must have been thrilled with the realization of such a spectacular achievement. Reveling in the crowd's wild roars of excitement and unusually loud cheering, Roy was violently tackled at the 1-yard line by his own teammate, who saved the game as Roy was about to score for the opposing team! A valuable course correction for Roy's team I would say. Sure, they had lost a lot of ground, but they still had a chance to make it up and start again in the right direction.

This is the core message of this book. Identifying wrong directions and motivating parents or future parents to make effective and necessary course corrections. In this book I present a fresh and previously unwritten perspective on parenting. Cutting through much of the modern jargon, I use powerful, personal anecdotes to explain how specific instruction from my parents helped my two brothers and me immensely.

Aside from my own experiences, I also refer to statistics, stories and observations of others to explain how many of my friends and many members of *Generation X* have been left to wander about and are now failing to find success. They were given plenty of food and shelter, but no real guidance and wisdom to carry them through the day-to-day responsibilities of life.

When these *Fair Warnings* are neglected by one or both parents, the odds for rearing truly successful children greatly diminish. The odds for raising children who continually make poor decisions in life greatly increase.

In effect, I am attempting to tackle any one of you who may be running unaware in the wrong direction. By neglecting to teach basic truths and provide *Fair Warnings* to our children, we are just like Roy Reigels who seemed to be experiencing the glory of his progress, only to be sorely disappointed when he realized the truth of his misguided efforts.

I remember a time when I dreaded taking my car to the shop because the awful noises, which bellowed from under the hood, convinced me that I could never afford the repairs that obviously needed to be made. Much to my surprise, after finally giving in to the howling within my hood, the mechanic reached deep within the engine and re-attached a disconnected valve. The cost? Only $10. This simple procedure eliminated the awful noises and relieved me of my haunting financial concerns.

Certainly, there are serious mechanical problems which occur despite our greatest efforts to maintain our vehicles. (I recently spent $1,600 on a new transmission!) But many costly repairs can be minimized or avoided through regular, proper maintenance.

We learn that small, consistent course corrections or *maintenance* will influence the ability of our children to choose the direction in life that they come naturally to know and feel is right, but many times lack the confidence and understanding to choose for themselves. We see that these same small and consistent course corrections will serve to provide motivation for our youth. They develop a desire to go forward as bridled, productive achievers rather than haphazard, aimless coasters. One such college graduate was recently asked, "So, what do you see yourself doing now that you are out of college?" He lethargically responded, "Uh, I'll probably just be working in the yard or fixing my car."

I have written this book not so much as a *step-by-step* or a *how-to*, but rather, as a thought-provoker and a motivator. It is my hope to provide you with some ideas, concepts, and truths that will serve to motivate those of you who are parents and those who will be parents. I hope that my views and experiences will motivate you to re-evaluate and deeply contemplate your life and the important role you have or will have as parents and builders of a great society.

I hope to stir your minds with logic and provide you with factual information about these *Fair Warnings*. Information about which most adults have long been aware, but may have allowed to lie dormant and buried in the rush of life or by the fetters of idleness. It is my hope that readers will come away from this book with a great desire to dedicate themselves to a quality family life and thus introduce themselves to their most dynamic and effective selves.

Finally, this book is designed to serve as a starting point for you to seek out more specific education, information and even instruction about personal change and spirituality from good authors, teachers, parents, and religious leaders who possess far more education and experience than myself.

Gordon B. Hinkley recently asked, "Do societies need more policemen? I do not dispute it. Do societies need more prisons? I suppose so. But what they need, above all else, is a strengthening of the homes of the people. Every child is a product of a home. Societies are having terrible youth problems, but I am convinced that they have a greater parent problem..." He continued, "What can be done? We cannot effect a turnaround in a day or a month or a year. But I am satisfied that with enough effort we can begin a turnaround within a generation and accomplish wonders within two generations. That is not a very long time in the history of man. There is nothing any of us can do that will have a greater long-term benefit than to rekindle wherever possible the spirit of the kind of homes in which goodness can flourish." (*Ensign*, Sep. 1996, pp.5)

You will come to find much happiness and satisfaction in your own life as you watch your posterity experience joy in their lives rather than mere temporary pleasures, followed by long-term failures and avoidable, self-inflicted hardship. Most of us possess a natural desire to make a positive and lasting impact on the lives of those we love so dearly, our families. As parents we are best able to warn our children about all things that we know to be destructive. If we will do this we will not only make our own "...*Good Children Great*," but we will also become "...*American Heroes*."

section

ONE

THE STATE OF THE UNION

CHAPTER 1:
Pit-Bulls and American Society

Historically, we see that a nation can survive a multiplicity of disasters, war, invasion, and disease, but no nation has ever been able to survive the disintegration of the family and the home.
                    -Lucille Johnson

July 18th, 1997. It was a picture perfect day in Laguna Beach, CA, only 11 days prior to my 26th birthday. Never in my wildest dreams would I have imagined I would be assaulted by a deadly Pit-Bull and a demented *Generation Xer* that day.

There I was, relaxing. Taking a break from the appointments of the day and taking advantage of one of my favorite locations. I sat on a bench overlooking the world-renowned Laguna Beach cove. That day hundreds of tourists and beachgoers were swarming about the beach, swimming in the surf, strolling along the boardwalk, eating lunch on the grass and watching the heated volleyball and basketball games. I had an hour to spare and was taking it all in and had settled down with a good book.

Suddenly my thoughts were interrupted by loud and ferocious barking. A Pit-Bull was attacking a Siberian Husky on a leash walking along with its master. I watched as the two dog owners struggled to separate the animals. The owner of the Pit-Bull, which was not on a leash, delivered several rapid blows with his fist to the head of his *beloved* pet while yelling at the top of his lungs for the dog to stop. Luckily the two men were able to separate them before the Pit-Bull had a chance to sink its teeth beyond the Husky's very dense coat.

I found myself annoyed that this dog-owner wasn't using enough common sense to have such an aggressive and over-whelmingly powerful animal on a leash. I soon found my annoyance increasing as I continued to watch the *master* beat his dog profusely in an attempt to scold the dog for doing exact-ly what it had been bred to do. When the beating ended, he hugged the dog, kissed it directly on the mouth and to my utter amazement, released the dog and again allowed it to sniff and wander about unleashed. The owner seemed oblivious to the many small children, hundreds of adults, and other animals in the area.

The young man who owned the dog appeared to be about 21 years old. He wore long shorts hanging so loosely that they rest-ed four or five inches below his waistline. His shorts were sag-ging, no doubt, because of the long silver chain which hung zoot-suit style from his back pocket to his front pocket. His bare torso revealed his sophisticated art collection, and his head was shaved nearly bald. Certainly the dog was an asset to his over-all image, and to actually leash the animal probably wasn't the coolest thing to do.

While I was thinking about the absurdity of it all, the Pit-Bull identified its next target and bolted across the grass toward a small white puppy. The owner chased the animal as fast as he could screaming for his dog to come back. No chance.

Luckily for the puppy, the Pit-Bull over-shot his target as he rapidly came upon the unsuspecting victim. The Pit-Bull was so excited and had moved so quickly that it ran right into the lit-tle dog, actually running it over and had to double back to get a hold of it. That gave the Pit-Bull's owner the split second he needed to dive across the grass and literally tackle his dog before it had a chance to successfully attack.

Another beating ensued and I was yet amazed that there was still no attempt to leash the dog and that this person made no effort to consider the safety of those around him.

I was now standing and watching as were many others. Being the type to speak up for what is right and appropriate, I cautiously walked near the owner. When I was within ear-shot, I said directly, but politely, "You know, a dog like that really ought to be on a leash in such a busy place. Somebody's bound to get hurt."

He had his back to me and was bent over, continuing to punish his large and muscular dog. He made no immediate response. He didn't even look my way. I was just about to move on when he quickly snatched up his dog under his right arm, turned and lunged toward me. As he jumped in my direction, and with a wild look in his eye and a terrible scowl on his face, he yelled at the top of his lungs, *"What did you say?! Do you want some of this dog, you blank-blank PUNK?"*

I backed away as fast as I could, stumbling as I had been caught off-guard. I found myself within inches of the snarling dog, (this happens to be one of the few domestic animals that strikes genuine fear in my heart) I answered calmly, "No, actually, I *don't* want any of your dog. I only asked that you put him on a leash." He continued to rush towards me yelling and screaming. He told me that he was going to let his dog loose on me, "How'd you like that...?" he asked sarcastically. He then explained that his dog would break my arm and tear up my leg. All of which I am certain he would have done. He taunted me and repeated again and again, "Come on, punk, let's fight right now! I'll kill you! You don't stand a chance you little..."

My heart pounded and I felt dizzied by the sudden rush of adrenaline. I felt as though I had no where to go. I couldn't run, surely the dog would catch me if it were let go. I couldn't fight back for fear that the dog would get hold of my arms and tear them to shreds. The owner wouldn't listen to reason, and he was relentless. I felt as though I were in a dream. Over 100 people had stopped, just watching and not saying a word. All that I could do was back away as fast as possible. I continued to back up in a continual stumble, holding my hand up in front of me, walking in a circle around and around repeating as loud as possible in between his threats and cursing, "Just get that dog away from me! Get that dog out of my face!" In an attempt to eliminate the possibility of being bitten, I suggested, "Why don't you put the dog away and handle me yourself?" Compared to the look in that dog's eyes, I had no fear of the coward who hid behind his animal.

After a minute of this merry-go-round, he slapped my forehead and knocked off my cap. I could do nothing but continue to back away from the dog. Then, he reached out and punched me in the arm, knocking the book out of my hand. I felt like the school-yard weakling about to get beat up by the bully!

In desperation, I looked out into the pathetic crowd and asked, "Are you guys going to just stand there and watch this or is somebody going to help me out with this dog here?" Nobody moved. I was flabbergasted.

Three or four minutes passed and the young man's aggression kept increasing. He apparently misinterpreted my constant running as a sign of my fear of *him*. It was as if his appetite to make good on his threats was increasing and the growing crowd only added fuel to his fire. He was swelling with pride and power.

I on the other hand, was horribly embarrassed. I felt as though I was the featured fight at the school bus stop. The situation had become ridiculous, and I could do nothing about it. What the bully didn't know is that, boys being boys, in years past, I had upon occasion had to take care of myself in similar situations.

Without warning, he handed the dog to a friend in the

crowd and charged towards me with a clenched fist. I had no time to run, negotiate, or even move. I simply waited for his punch and as it came at my face, I stepped to the side and delivered my own clenched fist of defense that landed hard, just above his eye and I followed up with a hard left into his other eye. His head flew back and he was spared the embarrassment of falling only because he was caught by some bystanders whom he stumbled into. Immediately a cheer rang out, and I looked in amazement at these spectators.

The loud-mouth held his hands over both eyes as he stumbled around. I backed away, wanting to have nothing to do with any of it. I reminded him, "Listen, I told you I didn't want to fight. I just defended myself!" He said nothing more and made no attempt to get near me. I picked up my hat and book and made my way through the crowd. Everyone gathered around, patting me on the back, telling me, "Great shot!" "Hey, you really nailed that maniac!" and "I saw it all, that guy was attacking you!" I kept my head down and thought to myself, "Yeah, then why didn't you do anything about it?"

What is happening to our society? Why was this kid so irresponsible and violent? Why are so few willing to stand up for what is right? Why are so few willing to assist someone who needs help? Why was it so strange to see the good guy win?

I found it interesting that the owner of the Pit-Bull became so angry and abusive when his dog attacked. After all, the animal was only doing what came naturally. The dog was doing exactly what it had been taught, having itself been abused by its master. Is there any question that the young man's violent behavior was also learned by example and grew because it was left unchecked?

I wonder if the parents of the children who witnessed our strange confrontation that day thought to take a minute or two to teach their kids something, anything about what had happened. Or were they just left to think that such events were acceptable and a normal part of public gatherings?

Lately, society is confronted by a terrible trend. Children are being taught bad behavior through the words and actions of their guardians and they are learning it from what surrounds them each day without parental intervention to illustrate what is best for them. Rarely does someone learn to have a positive outlook and a productive attitude without the direct influence of someone helping that come about.

Consider the direction of many within my generation. One *Generation X* college student recently concluded a speech to hundreds of students with this statement, "...we now have nothing to look forward to!" He had just outlined the ills of society and explained how the opportunities available to the previous generation no longer exist. His words were received with thunderous applause.

Excuse me? Who told him *that?* And why were those people applauding such a statement? I know that I only applaud those things with which I agree or at least appreciate. So why did this particular audience of *Generation Xers* enthusiastically agree with such a dismal and limiting message? What does this say about the future of America?

Our Founding Fathers were faced with seemingly insurmountable odds at the inception of this great country. What would have happened if they had believed that it was simply too difficult to forge ahead and decided that there was nothing to look forward to in the face of such opposition? Would we have ever known the freedoms that we enjoy and the opportunities that that freedom makes possible?

Many of my generation have been taught that they have, in effect, "...nothing to look forward to." The result? The slacker segment of *Generation X*. Misguided, disinterested, and hooked on MTV.

Douglas Rushkoff, a popular author of that segment of the *X* generation, has written in his book, *The Gen X Reader*, that *Generation X* (referred to as Busters) has been, "Born into a society where traditional templates have proven themselves quaint at best, and mass-murderous at worst. Busters feel liberated from the constraints of ethical systems, but also somewhat cast adrift. It must be nice to have something external to believe in. Having no such permanent icon (no God, no Country, no Superhero) we choose instead, by default, actually, to experience life as play..." He further writes, "...we see our increasing apathy as a strength and make a *conscious effort* to teach our compatriots how to remain liberated from the mind-numbing...hypnotic demagoguery perpetuated so successfully on everybody else....*whether you like it or not, we are the thing that will replace you.*" A very frightening thought!

On the other hand, we find many *Generation Xers* who are seething with ambition and hope. One *Generation X* website (www.jollyroger.com) reads, "We're proud to be the voice of the contemplating *Generation Xers*, inspired by truths higher than heroin, preferring thinking to drinking and mowing the grass to smoking it. We're cultural mutineers; guardians of common sense..."

In June 1997, *TIME* ran a lengthy article on *Generation X* by Margot Hornblower. Hornblower explains that, "They (twenty-somethings) may be cynical about institutions, but they remain remarkably optimistic as individuals. At least half believe that they will be better off financially than their parents. And an astonishing 96% of *Gen Xers* say, 'I am very sure that one day I will get to where I want to be in life.'—showing far more confidence than Boomers did a generation ago. For all their ironic detachment, today's young adults embrace an American dream—albeit one different from the vision their parents or grandparents had."

Without question, this is a fragmented group. Too young for any real accurate classification and too new to be completely understood. But what *Generation X* certainly does share is this, we were raised in world of social decline and unstable foundations, which has heavily clouded the minds of many in regard to an overall understanding of morality or the need for principle-centered living. Most of us were raised by the Baby Boomers and by their own admission, the Boomers didn't do much to improve our familial and social strengths. In the same *TIME* article, "...pollsters find that Boomers are markedly more pessimistic than Xers. Fully 71% of Boomers say, 'If I had the chance to start over in life, I would do things differently.'"

Mona Charen wrote in the June 22, 1997 edition of *The Washington Times*, "We have engaged, since the great feminist revolution of the 1960s, in a wholesale retreat from child-rearing...The evidence is all around us that children are terribly damaged by the neglect they've suffered these past 30 years. Promiscuous divorce, illegitimacy and, yes, overwork by parents have combined to create a society in which children are left to raise themselves."

And so today, we are at a crossroads. A changing of the guard. The last of the Boomers are raising their children and the *Generation Xers* are just starting their families. I wonder what my generation; a mixture of low ambition and bursting, unbridled ambition, is planning to teach their children? Are they even making any plans? And what are our present day parents of teens teaching right now?

One thing I am sure of is this: Most children eventually become as their parents are. Just as the Pit-Bull took its violent lead from its master. Children learn and carry on the *traditions of the fathers* as a whole. And of late, many parents haven't been, well, going the extra mile!

The result in today's society is that we are now witnessing the perpetuation of the *If-it-feels-good, do-it!* attitude. It is all around us; and if this continues from generation to generation, we are headed for a very painful and eventually irreversible social dilemma.

William Bennett in his book, *The Index of Leading Cultural Indicators*, points out, "A disturbing and telling sign of the declining condition among the young is evident in an on-going survey. Over the years teachers have been asked to identify the top problems in America's public schools. In 1940, teachers identified talking out of turn, chewing gum, making noise, running in the halls, cutting in line, dress code infractions, and littering. When asked the same question in 1990, teachers identified drug use, alcohol abuse, pregnancy, suicide, rape, robbery, and assault."

Societal decay is gaining momentum at a shocking rate, and we are seeing this downward spiral increase in pitch and velocity as if to foretell the probability of a complete flat spin in the near future. The day has come, and our children are facing personal, familial, and educational problems far more difficult than we may have ever imagined. If this generational spiral is left uncorrected, following generations will be left to stand alone, and lacking knowledge, will certainly perish.

Upsetting, yes. But please, take heart! We have not yet arrived at that point! Despite all that we see that is disappointing, our social problems are not irreversible. We are not in a flat spin at this point, and I happen to believe that the majority of the people in this world are trying to do what they believe is right. There is an abundance of happiness and opportunity to be found each day. Life in America remains full of many luxuries and possibilities, which cannot be found anywhere else in the world. As we experience this looming concern for the future of our society and for the world, the need to begin making necessary and truly effective course corrections becomes urgent. It is now that we need to extend the *Fair Warnings* that the next generation deserves to be made aware of.

I love to surf, read, listen to good music, and dance around the house with my wife and kids. In addition to experiencing life's joys, I am a concerned parent and citizen. I have watched many of my own peers stumble through life when perhaps some of their flailings could have been avoided. As I have talked to many friends and acquaintances about the degree of guidance they received in their homes (and finding in some cases that guidance was virtually non-existent!), I am convinced that to change the direction of this country, many specific familial changes must be made. There is an obvious and urgent need for concerned and participating parents. Parents who are not only concerned with insisting their kids wear helmets when riding bikes, eat right, wash behind their ears, and avoid bad men in slow moving vehicles, but who also insist their children are taught specific rules and truths about life as well; rules or principles such as honesty, hard work, positive attitude, and kindness. In short, we need great leaders.

Only after more leaders of families emerge and this change occurs will the *Pit-Bulls* of American society, which threaten the welfare of children, begin to lose their strength. Only then will we see more happiness in each home. Only then will more and more parents witness their children reach their full potential.

section
TWO

THE ROLE OF PARENTS

CHAPTER 2:

The Most Powerful Position In America

The courageous man finds a way, the ordinary man finds an excuse.
- Author Unknown

Recently on a talk show a disgruntled mother complained about the release of new statistics indicating that drug use among teens is soaring again reflecting nearly the high percentages of the 70s and early 80s.

"If this President hadn't been elected, this would have never happened!" she proclaimed. "So what you're saying," asked the host "is that our President is solely to blame for our national drug problem?" "Well not solely," she answered. "But it's also the fault of the citizens who voted him in. I mean, after all, we do put him up there as our babies' example, don't we?"

Now do we really believe, whether we agree or disagree with any particular President, during a four to eight year period, this is the *one* individual immediately responsible for little Johnny's heroin problem?

Without question, the policies of an administration can significantly impact economic and national security issues. Social issues, however, are not so immediately influenced by any administration's politics.

Over the years social problems such as drug use, sexual promiscuity, and the devaluation of human life can be and may be nurtured and promoted by laws passed and political agendas, which slowly but surely work their way through the system. But these laws are only fertilizer, feeding the roots of social problems planted years before within the walls of the American home. Certainly, we do our best to elect men and women who represent the good in America. We attempt to elect those whom we honestly believe stand for correct principles when we cast our votes. But do we really put them up there as this good woman indicated "...as our babies' examples?"

Certainly with time, political leaders do have an opportunity to influence youth for good or ill. They do have an impact on our social temperature depending upon the policies they accept or reject. However, there is no excuse for any parent in this country to lay the blame for their own children's problems including teen-age pregnancy or a life-long criminal career at the feet of politicians, school districts and voters. Political policies only add fertilizer to the roots of all individuals who are ultimately *home grown*.

In the same vein, John Engler, Governor of Michigan, recently stated, "The wisdom of the ages reveals that our moral compass cannot ultimately come from Lansing or from any other state capital, any more than it can come from the nation's capital, or Hollywood, or the United Nations... It comes from deep within us, it comes from our character, which is forged in our families and our faith and tempered in the arena of decision-making and action."

Every child is born pure. Although children do arrive with various genetic traits, none are born destined to success or failure. None are consigned to a life of crime. None are guaranteed they will be an instant success. But all are guaranteed the opportunity for either. History is replete with stories of individuals born with all of the worldly ease and comfort available to them, who end up in prison or lead lives of self-inflicted scandal and controversy. Good looks, a proper education, and the financial independence to enjoy in a free country are not enough to breed a champion. Likewise, history is full of tremendous stories of individuals who began their lives in poverty and pain, yet rose to become great and contributing members of their society. They grew up on dirt floors. Many were allowed to attend school until only the fourth grade because they had to work every day to assist their families. Their economic and social opportunities were severely limited. They were surrounded by hardship and crime. Yet, these people chose a course in life that was rich and fulfilling. They rose above their trying environment.

Why were these individuals able to succeed amid such opposition, while others met failure after growing up under what are considered ideal circumstances? I think of Howard Hughes who experienced years of incredible financial success, public praise, and a glamorous lifestyle. Ironically, Mr. Hughes lived out his final days as a recluse. It is reported that he spent day after day alone watching old films and passing the time in idle and destructive behavior. He traded his handsome features for an unkempt beard and a decrepit, unfit body. He finally died quietly, alone, and admittedly miserable.

Why? Why was he not satisfied with all he had achieved? All the financial independence one could desire. Were his habits and depression too great to overcome? Why did he fall to the depths of depression? Was it the President's fault? Why did he choose destructive behavior? Did the schools forget to teach him about proper mental health and lifelong achievement? Did the public attention bring him down?

Ana Quirot was born in poverty in Cuba. Armed with a natural born will to win, she became a national hero after winning the bronze metal in the 800- meter run during the 1992 Olympics. Becoming an Olympic medalist revealed her strength and depth of character. It goes without saying that this is a highly honorable and rare achievement. An unexpected accident later proved to magnify her deeper level of greatness.

While cooking in her kitchen in January of 1993, Ana was overtaken in a sudden grease fire, which quickly spread burning major portions of her body. While in the hospital fighting for her life, she gave birth prematurely to a daughter who died after a week. Having been dealt this terrible tragedy and left disabled, much of the tissue on her legs and arms was severely burned dramatically altering her appearance; it was automatically assumed that her career as a runner was finished. She may run again, some thought, but never at the world class level. This was the assumption of the general public, but she thought otherwise.

Prior to this unforeseen event, Ana had set her sights on another Olympic competition. With this original goal still in mind and relatively little time to prepare, she began a rigorous program to achieve complete rehabilitation. Seemingly unaffected by the odds stacked against her and willing to continue to feel beautiful in spite of the fact that her face was severely scarred and changed for life, she continued with confidence and maintained the determination necessary to achieve her goal. To the astonishment of the world but probably not to those who knew her best, she did indeed achieve her goal. She began her comeback in November of 1993, running the 800 meters in 2:03.19 and placing second in the Central American Games. Again she became the top in her country, winning the nationals in 1995. She represented Cuba in the 1996 Olympic games and experienced the joy and sweet satisfaction of realizing this magnificent and very rarely achieved goal.

How did she do it? And why? Who influenced her attitude toward life? Was it a charitable Cuban government policy that taught her success? Did she receive a large financial subsidy as her motivation? No.

The answer to these questions lies in the fact that somewhere along the way Ana, and others who succeed are taught a vital truth of life. This truth of life is that everyone is born with a wonderful tool that we must learn to use carefully throughout our lives. It is the gift of agency. The power to act for ourselves. We have the mental freedom to choose our way in life. To exert the same amount of effort toward personal happiness as Ana Quirot did in her quest for the Olympics. Thoreau said, "I know of no more encouraging fact than the unquestionable ability of man to elevate his life by conscious endeavor."

Relatively few people have the physical ability and mental strength to become Olympic athletes. On the other hand, there is only a minuscule group of people, when compared to the whole, who do not possess the ability and mental capacity to create a wealth of happiness and success in their own personal lives.

We literally create happiness or difficulty as a result of our decisions and reactions to the multitude of circumstances in our lives. Except in the case of severe mental and physical incapacity there is not a single situation in life in which we are not able to decide what our reaction or response will be. These reactions and responses are literally what shape and fashion our character or who we become. As we make correct and productive choices day-to-day, our ability to continue in this direction is strengthened. Likewise, if we choose the lesser part, our ability to recognize and choose the good becomes more limited and opaque.

Consider the following quotation as it applies to our thoughts, whether good or bad; they eventually define our condition in life. "Let a man radically alter his thoughts and he will be astonished at the rapid transformation it will effect in the material conditions in his life. Men imagine that thought can be kept in secret, but it cannot; it rapidly crystallizes into habit, and a habit solidifies into circumstance."

Whether our actions are good or bad, Ralph Waldo Emerson points out, "That which we persist in doing becomes easier. Not that the nature of the task has changed, but our ability to do has increased." Our habits, good or bad, become easier and easier as we practice them.

If our parents or guardians do not understand this truth, how will it be learned? Are we going to wait and make vain attempts to teach these principles after our children are teens, and we see that we are losing them? In answer to a question in a survey, which I distributed among college students, a 20 year-old girl attending UC Davis indicates that, "I feel that a lot of the decisions I've made about my life (i.e., not to smoke, drink, cheat, etc.) have been the result of the values instilled in me by my parents."

Are we willing to risk the chances of our children learning the necessary principles in school alone? Show me a school district that carefully and lovingly teaches these principles every day beginning in pre-school and extends the lessons through high school. They cannot. They are not intended for that purpose and are not equipped to do so. I have heard of supposed *unified* school districts, none which provide the unity necessary to raise our children with consistent principled teaching. Sure, there are many fantastic instructors throughout the country. Loving, concerned and wise teachers, coaches, and religious leaders who have a life-long impact on our children and even serve as a father or mother figure when the parents are not more available. Sometimes this happens, but in most cases it is friends and other pressures that become the overriding influence in the absence of good parenting. We all know and have seen the results when children lead children or when adults who were raised without direction lead children down crooked paths. Let's look at the principle of agency a little further to see how it literally creates a wealth of opportunity when correctly applied or weaves a web that binds when left unchecked and ignored.

We read about and are aware of the difficulty kicking a drug habit. I have been told that nicotine ranks right up there with heroine and cocaine in terms of difficulty when attempting to quit after an extended period of use. Each of us knows someone who abuses alcohol who has not mustered the strength to quit but has made the attempt time and time again. There are millions of smokers who vow to kick their habit on New Year's Day. I'll bet the majority of those millions break their promise within two or three days.

To spawn this or any destructive and hard-to-break habit, people experience a day in which they disregard an initial gut feeling. They ignore that whisper in their ear which says, in effect, "You'd better not do this. This is not the right thing to do!" We have all heard that little voice. Some call it a conscience. Others call it our Guardian Angel, The Holy Ghost or The Spirit. At some other point while deciding to take that first puff, some may flatly ignore these promptings and later can scarcely even recall the initial, inner advice. Others may fight a little battle within their soul before deciding because somewhere within they know they have been taught they should not experiment with cigarettes. They know it is bad for them. All make the choice either to heed or ignore the directive of that companion for good within each of us. The personal vices that trouble hundreds of thousands of Americans began months or years ago when the choice was made to ignore the initial warnings.

Over time, those who choose to continue smoking, for example, literally force their way through the unpleasant coughing and gasping stage and are finally deaf to the wise whisperings, which initially warned them to avoid such things. Now their ability to step away and move in another direction is greatly hindered as a result of their own free will and choice. In time most clearly recognize the growth and imminent danger of this habit. Some decide it is time to overcome this habit. Much to their dismay, they find they are now facing not only a large mental obstacle but also a physical one. Their bodies have become accustomed to and dependent upon the stimulating effects created by their indulgence or their drug of choice: nicotine, alcohol, or cocaine, to name a few. Their ability to choose, or agency, is now hindered in this area because the habit has been practiced to the point at which many feel that it is nearly impossible to quit. Clinically referred to as addictions. I simply call them nasty habits.

The word, addiction, is usually linked to drug use and occasionally to deviant sexual behavior. I suggest that *any* negative or compulsive behavior in our lives we choose to grow and continue to feed falls into this category. The only difference is that the lesser perpetual behaviors are usually called bad habits. The more severe and physically destructive vices are referred to as addictions. It is all the same, only some are much harder to correct than others.

These bad habits are always connected to some sort of temporary pleasure or gratification, which requires virtually no effort on the part of the participant to enjoy. Virtually anyone can achieve the desired effect. Once the initial struggle to decide to indulge is resolved all one needs to do is inhale, swallow or snort the chemical. Simple. And so it goes with stealing, lying, gossiping, or being unkind. To steal we pick up something we want and take it without asking or paying for it. Lying is as simple as breathing itself. Violence is achieved with the mere swing of a fist. And feelings are torn with one sharp word.

Alexander Pope penned it well when he wrote in his *An Essay on Man*:

> *Vice is a monster of so frightful mien,*
> *As to be hated needs but to be seen;*
> *But seen too oft, familiar with it's face,*
> *We first endure, then pity, then embrace.*

As soon as we decide to involve ourselves in any form of negative behavior, we open the door to repetition. It becomes easier and easier to repeat. The second drink is much easier than the first. The first theft is accompanied by much more worry and nervousness than the next. The first time we verbally lash out at our parents in rebellion is accompanied by much more adrenaline and fear than the second and third such event. We set ourselves up for more and more habitual behavior. We lose our sensitivity to our conscience and continue to weave a web of problems for ourselves and inevitably those around us.

Sir Winston Churchill once said, "A nation without a conscience is a nation without a soul. A nation without a soul is a nation that cannot live." Some choose a course fraught with difficulty and despair only to finally wonder, while sitting in a jail cell, in a re-hab center, out of a job, without friends, without family, without hope, "Why did this happen to me?" As more and more individuals ask that question amid their personal, self-inflicted dilemmas, the collective voice of this country will soon whine in that same tone, "How could this have happened to us?"

So many young people are left to realize the results of their behavior only after experiencing these hardships. They are easily enticed by the fun of drinking and drug use. They are easily influenced by the thrill and ease of stealing. Teenage sex gives a false sense of maturity and status. It becomes second nature to show disrespect and exhibit vulgarity. And why not? Without anything else to look to, why wouldn't this be the natural course for many of them? It is all around them. With the help of certain media and the mass of peer involvement, it all appears so fun to any of us with so little experience. And initially, it is fun. How does anyone possibly recognize the real danger and impact of their behavior without leadership from someone who knows?

Socrates wisely once asked, "Whom, then, do I call educated? First, those who control circumstances instead of being mastered by them; those who meet all occasions manfully and act in accordance with intelligent thinking; those who are honorable in all dealings, who treat good-naturedly persons and things that are disagreeable; and furthermore, those who hold their pleasures under control and are not overcome by misfortune."

The people who live without such vices have no need to complain, "Why did all of this happen to me?" They know exactly why those things have not happened to them. The happy, productive, and achieving people made a conscious and specific decision to move forward not backward. They are properly educated about life. They have the presence of mind to follow their inner prompting to do what is right. When they make mistakes, they are able to learn from them and begin to change. These people are willing to delay immediate gratification for greater, long-term rewards. If bad habits are sown, they know there is no habit or weakness too great to overcome. They know that drug use can be curbed. Stealing, lying, and cheating are character traits, which with the required determination can be overcome. They know that to endure the pain of ridicule, the difficulty of self-restraint, and the passing up of a temporary pleasure are necessary for growth, maturity, confidence, and true happiness. They understand they can choose to respond to any situation in a positive way. They control emotions and appetites at will. They are sure they can correct situations when they have done wrong. They rise above their own personal nightmares in life just as Ana Quirot was able to do. They were given *Fair Warning* early on and learned these valuable truths through the words and more significantly by the example of one or both parents.

The truth about the pathway to success or failure is depicted so well in the words of this anonymous quotation entitled *Habit*:

> *I am your constant companion. I am your greatest helper or heaviest burden.*
>
> *I will push you onward or drag you down to failure. I am completely at your command. Half the things you do you might just as well turn over to me and I will be able to do them quickly and correctly.*
>
> *I am easily managed - you must merely be firm with me. Show me exactly how you want something done and after a few lessons I will do it automatically.*
>
> *I am the servant of all great men; and alas of all failures, as well. Those who are great, I have made great. Those who are failures, I have made failures.*
>
> *I am not a machine, though I work with all the precision of a machine plus the intelligence of a man. You may run me for profit or run me for ruin-it makes no difference to me.*
>
> *Take me, train me, be firm with me, and I will place the world at your feet. Be easy with me and I will destroy you.*
>
> *WHO AM I? I AM HABIT!*

I was an unusually small kid. I looked like a large toddler up until the sixth grade. Nevertheless, I always seek out adventure. My older brothers, Greg and Chris, were always seeking ways to experiment and test their adventures on me. One day when I was about 11 years-old and Chris was 15, he and I came up with a neat idea.

In the garage, we found a cardboard produce box in which I could snugly fit. It seemed like we had found a neat boxcar/plane for me to ride in. Literally. We put the box on top of an old skateboard. Chris was going to give me a running push with a final heave-ho down our sloping cul-de-sac.

This was sure to be exhilarating. Exhilarating for me because of the speed and rushing wind; for Chris because of the element of danger with virtually no physical risk for himself whatsoever. He didn't even need to coax me. I was eager for the adventure. At that age, he was a little sharper than I.

We put the skateboard in place at the top of the street. Alone with the street clear of moving vehicles, all systems were go. Chris held the box steady on top of the skateboard as I stepped in. My hips tightly slid in as I sat down. I sat with my knees bent, pulled up close to my chest, arms wrapped around the front of my shins to squeeze nicely into the cardboard.....cockpit. The top of the ...um, *cockpit* rose to my shoulders, only my little blonde head looking forward was revealed. I was ready to ride!

I gave Chris the thumbs up, and he started the engines. A slow jog at first to build momentum. His legs.....my engines ran faster as we hit a slight decline. I began to experience the thrill of our trial run. Soon we were at full throttle and ready to add the most excitement (or entertainment) possible. He gave that final burst of power, the old heave-ho. I would coast alone at top speed down the rest of the street, surely to hop out after our successful mission and sprint back to the top for another *flight*.

Prior to Chris' final heave-ho, unbeknownst to us, the *cock-pit* had slowly rattled its way to the very front edge of the skateboard. With that last power burst, the *cockpit* unfortunately took the plunge. Together, we plunged right off the front of the craft while traveling at top speed. Arms secured inside, I couldn't free them to use as a brace. Inertia fully in tact, our momentum met with a sudden thud. The weighed down cardboard meeting rough asphalt resulted in an even quicker halt. The texture of the cardboard eliminated any sliding possibility. Brilliant engineering design. After the initial thud as the street grabbed the cardboard upon impact, there was only one appendage available as the final braking system to bring the disconnected bird to its final resting place. This would be the skinny neck along with the sandy blonde head, which peered valiantly, wide-eyed, out of the cockpit. And braking system I was. I ended the flight face first into the pavement.

Luckily, I only suffered the loss of one or two layers of skin on my forehead, nose, and right cheek. To this day I still wonder how I didn't lose my nose altogether! Chris thought we should give it just one more try. I declined.

If we had been so fortunate as to have had an adult spying on us that day, I would have been spared some pain and suffering. I also would have had a more handsome school picture in my photo album from that year!

I feel it is safe to assume that prior to this particular crash and burn and under these circumstances, most responsible adults would have recognized the imminent dangers and said something to make us aware of our stupidity. Ironic, when we felt, well...ingenious. Just one quick phrase or warning might have forced us to step back and at least evaluate the project.

Now, not being very savvy back then, I might have considered the frailties of our vehicle, but in the excitement of the moment decided that the show must still go on. There was just no time to waste. But then again, I might very well have taken these precautions into consideration and, out of concern for my own well-being, made some modifications.

I could have secured the box to the skateboard somehow and tried a little test run down the driveway first. I could have freed my arms from being so tightly tucked around my legs, totally prohibiting any movement and greatly inhibiting balance. Whether I chose to heed the advice or not, my odds for success and added safety could have immediately increased 100-fold.

How many far more dangerous, real-life situations will our own children come up against? Whether they heed them or not, who is going to give the needed words of caution? Who really possesses the most powerful position in America? I say it is me. I have the most power in America. I am merely 26 years old, but I am a father. Because of that responsibility, I wield the greatest power in this entire country! If you are a father or mother or plan to be one, then you possess the same power as well.

I accept the responsibility. I will not wait for others to do my job for me. I do not hold school districts or federal budgets responsible for the future of my children.

My wonderful wife, Shana, also wields this power. To an even greater degree, mothers, I believe, always carry more weight with their kids when they lead well because she carried them. She's simply mom. Together, we make family decisions, and these carry more weight than the numerous bills passed in majestic congressional halls. Over time, our correct decisions in family leadership will have more effect on the good of our society than 100 State of the Union addresses.

Likewise, I accept that if I choose to abdicate my powerful position by neglecting to guide my children well, I will play a major role in the destruction of this country. I have the power to do that. I recognize that an overall societal and generational decline in character will destroy more than a nuclear holocaust or natural disaster.

As parents or future parents, together we will rejoice in the results of our leadership or weep as we wish we had been more true to our responsibilities. We are the only ones who can teach a young child about the real dangers he/she inevitably will face. An occasional warning at school or church will not be enough to weather the constant, daily barrage of enticements our children confront. Good times and financial ease combined with casual instruction are not enough. Less than a 10 or 15 minute conversation with our children each day is not sufficient. No child care facility is qualified to bear your instructional responsibilities. Unexplained, unbending strictness does not breed obedience. Punishment without purpose does not breed trust. An abundant allowance of premature and unearned freedoms will create a loss of parental leverage. Acts of emotional; physical; and the most abhorrent, sexual abuse turns a bright, gifted child to sadness and despair. These children find their ability to make correct decisions for a successful future hindered. The lives of their children are at risk even before birth.

Boyd K. Packer shares this story in a talk entitled, *Problems in Teaching the Moral Standard*, "I recall on one occasion, when I was returning to my home for lunch that as I drove in my wife met me in the driveway. I could tell from the expression on her face that something was wrong. 'Cliff has been killed,' she said. 'They want you to come over.' As I hastened around the corner where Cliff lived with his wife and four sons and his little daughter, I saw Cliff lying in the middle of the highway with a blanket over him. The ambulance was just pulling away with little Colleen. Cliff had been on his way out to the farm and had stopped to cross the street to take little Colleen to her mother who waited on the opposite curb. But the child, as children will, broke from her father's hand and slipped into the street. A large truck was coming. Cliff jumped from the curb and pushed his little daughter from the path of the truck...but he wasn't soon enough.

"A few days later I had the responsibility of talking at the funeral of Cliff and little Colleen. Someone said, 'What a terrible waste. Certainly he ought to have stayed on the curb. He knew the child might have died. But he had four sons and a wife to provide for. What a pathetic waste!' And I estimated that that individual never had had the experience of loving someone more than he loved himself."

In the heat of the moment, I believe most parents will sacrifice their lives to rescue or protect their children from physical danger or death. It is a natural reaction to jump into action when life-threatening events occur. Yet, many parents stand on the curb of life and watch as their children are mowed over before their very eyes. They are mowed over by the life-threatening obstacles and trials of life which bound toward them each day. Because it is a more gradual tragedy, we procrastinate, rationalize or altogether overlook the need to sacrifice ourselves on behalf of our young ones.

We may not be called upon literally to sacrifice our lives as Cliff was, but we must sacrifice much on a daily basis if we are to save the lives of America's youth. It is requisite that we live up to our position of power and stop wishing things to change. And stop worrying that other organizations do not provide adequate education and instruction. We must break the habit of looking at institutional reliance as the cure for society's problems and turn our hearts and efforts to the only true societal vaccine, which I refer to as familial self-reliance. We must be willing to sacrifice our personal bad habits and spend more of our time, talents,   financial comfort, recreation, and excess leisure, on behalf of our children. If we are to reverse our present course, we must learn to truly love our children more than we love ourselves.

As we do these things, I believe it is inevitable that our youth will consider the impact of their decisions with greater sensitivity and more often choose the good. Gangs will diminish, drug use will decline, violent crime will lessen, divorce rates will decrease, physical abuse will be curbed, far fewer infants will be born illegitimately, depression will be supplanted with satisfaction and peace, economies will flourish, educators will excel, politicians will be less pliable, prison walls will no longer burst with over-population, welfare rolls will be rolled back, and tabloid magazines will be extinct.

May we wield our power wisely and take counsel from Henry David Thoreau who said, "The fate of the country...does not depend on what kind of paper you drop into the ballot box once a year, but on what kind of man you drop from your chamber into the street every morning."

CHAPTER 3:

No Greater Joy, No Greater Achievement.

When you want a thing bad enough to go out and fight for it, to work day and night for it, to give up your peace and your sleep and your time for it, if only the desire   that makes your aim strong enough never to tire of it; If life seems all empty and useless without it, and all that you dream and you scheme is about it, if simply you'll go after the thing that you want with all your capacity, strength and sagacity, faith, hope and confidence, stern pertinacity; if neither poverty, nor cold, nor famish and gaunt, nor sickness or pain of body and brain, can turn you away from the aim that you want, if dogged and grim you beseech and beset it, YOU'LL GET IT!

- Author Unknown

While arranging the multitude of details for our wedding, we felt that the quality of our DJ would add greatly to the mood of our reception. We hoped to find someone who would represent our style of music and enjoyment and help our guests feel comfortable and entertained. I have a friend with much experience as a DJ who has a nice, casual way about him. But Nancy, my fantastic, soon-to-be mother-in-law, had a friend, whose brother's wife knew a guy who had heard about a friend's wedding where the DJ was pretty good. Nancy was footing the rather large wedding tab, and this DJ's price sounded right. The fifth-hand source seemed acceptable, and so it was a done deal. We found the all important DJ.

Now we did have a few basic and minor requests. 1) No long-winded, unsolicited speeches, 2) no hula hoops, 3) no personal stories, 4) no Saturday Night Fever music, 5) no *Achy*

Breaky Heart, 6) no Barry Manilow, 7) no Air Supply, 8) no solo musical renditions, 9) stick to the basic music list we provided, and 10) no smoking.

Finally, the long awaited day had come! Just after our wedding ceremony and pictures, we arrived at Shana's grandfather's home in Studio City, CA for the reception. We rested for an hour or two as the final preparations were made.

While casually talking and relaxing in the backyard, I thought to myself, "Did I just see what I think I did?" I took a second look and sure enough, I had. Hula hoops! There was a very short, bearded man in his mid-50s wearing auto-tint sunglasses with a nearly fireproof polyester suit walking very briskly across the dance floor to the DJ booth. Over his shoulder he confidently carried three brightly colored hula hoops. He was obviously ready to groove the night away, to pull out all the stops.

The guests arrived and were bustling about happily in the yard as they found their seats and got situated. The florist, still wearing her work clothes, struggled to get through the crowd and set the centerpieces (promised much earlier in the day) on the tables. Working hard and obviously stressed with her tardiness, we noticed perspiration dripping from her brow occasionally as she placed each centerpiece just so. Meanwhile, our well-intentioned DJ was giving orders in an effort to help match up the wedding party couples for their formal introduction. Amidst our excited chatter in a narrow hallway as we awaited the introductions, an angry, "HEY! GET IN LINE AND LISTEN UP!" startled us all. I can't recall anything else our disciplinarian DJ said, but I do remember he was very angry with my excited whisperings, and I was almost excused from my own wedding party line. Now, that would have been a bad thing for us all; especially considering how long Shana and I had waited for this very exciting day! It would have been the first wedding reception at which a groom was banished to the guest area for talking out of turn.

The introductions commenced. Each couple was introduced to our friends and family, while what sounded like an action scene from a 1974 *Charlie's Angel's* instrumental disco sound-track blared in the background. At last, he declared, "It is my proud privilege to introduce to you, your host and hostess for this evening, Mr. and Mrs. Jeffrey Cheves!!" (My ethnicity went from Mexican to French in one fell swoop.) As we started walking from the hallway toward the entrance to the backyard, his chosen theme song filled the air. My stomach sank as I recognized that it was none other than the *Rocky* theme song, you know the one. We felt as though we should have been running up the stairs of city hall with our guests cheering wildly as they ran behind us. In fact, as we made our pass around the dance floor I found myself mouthing the words "GETTING STRONG NOW...," while looking around for a rack of raw ribs to slam my fist against!

As the evening progressed, the DJ veered further and further from the contract. We did hear a long Armenian folk tale which was a breach of contract: line 1) No long-winded, unsolicited speeches. There was also a breach of contract pertaining to the music list. He had his own top 100 to play. As a result, the dance floor sustained 80% vacancy for the better part of the evening. He did, however, get our first song correct...well, the title at least. I think Billy Joel sings *She's Got a Way About Her* better than anyone. After all, it is his song. Our version was sung by some other talented artist. It was O.K. We just had the feeling that we were dancing at a karaoke competition. As if that were not enough, the DJ smoked like a chimney (another contractual breach). And for the record, he was quietly asked to

NO GREATER JOY, NO GREATER ACHIEVEMENT

forego the hula hoop game. He obliged.

Now I can joke about our DJ and his inability to meet the contract terms in good fun. These are the days in life we look back on with great fondness and laughter. We all had a great time. I know he did. In fact, he made a new friend whom we think he went out with after. She was the one in the form-fitting black dress nobody seemed recognize. Finally we came to realize that it was our overworked florist who was wise enough to bring a change of clothes and stick around for the meal. It was a happy ending for all.

Our wedding day was the greatest day of our lives. For years each of us had waited and wondered whom we would marry, and what it would be like. We had excitedly prepared for our wedding for many months after finding each other. It was the first milestone in our life together. For us it was a deeply spiritual experience. We entered our marriage firm in our belief that our union will last throughout eternity if we both honor our marriage covenants. We had started a great new chapter in our lives with friends and family with their love and support. No DJ could change that. No previous experience or achievement could overshadow it. It was a defining moment. A moment nearly all people on the face of the earth look forward to and dream of experiencing in one form or another, sooner or later.

A few weeks ago a friend of mine pointed out an advertisement he noticed in a playbill for a popular play in the LA area. It was an ad for a popular make of a luxury cars. Along with a beautiful picture of the vehicle, this company included a list of 20 of the greatest experiences in a lifetime. Obviously, included on this checklist is driving this particular vehicle. Other events on the list include: 5. Wear a suit made by a Seville tailor, 8. See the sun rise at Machu Picchu, Peru, 10. Fly on the Concord, 11. Stand on the Great Wall of China, 12. Make

[53]

your own beer, 15. Take a balloon ride over the Serenghetti, 17. Kiss passionately in public, and number 19. Ride the rapids of the Snake River in Idaho.

Truly exciting and adventurous experiences. I would enjoy many of them. I found it interesting though, that among this list of greatest experiences in life there was no mention of marriage. No mention of the birth of a child, a baptism or bar mitzvah. No reference to birthday parties, basketball games and the ballet. What about the Tooth Fairy, Santa Clause, and Disneyland? No inclusion of prom night, graduations, college acceptances, engagements and marriages. Nor any mention of anniversaries, family vacations or reunions.

These *are* the truly great experiences of life. These are the milestones, the defining moments. Included in any family's history you will find that these are the greatest days, the fondest memories. In the great stories about these days, millions of families share their stories about memorable individuals, DJs and others, who add humor and uniqueness to events, making them not only spiritual and deeply moving , but also fun, sometimes hilarious and absolutely unforgettable. These experiences seem to perpetually overflow and lead to many long and oft-repeated reflections with friends and family which begin with "Remember when...?!"

Millions of couples enjoy the beauty and excitement of their wedding day. And many of those millions enjoy two, three or even 10 years of good times coupled with moderate marital and familial success. But approximately half of the married couples in America do not make it to the end hoped for on that memorable wedding day. One or both are not willing to pay the price for such success. One or both seek material things that seem to bring greater happiness. One or both are not willing to learn to work through problems and create the invaluable growth and experience they would have gained had they the willingness to change, contribute and endure. They miss out on years of milestone moments and create a most difficult and heartbreaking situation for the spouse who, in many cases, may have been willing to do his/her part. Much more significant though, they leave their children in broken homes adding more mountains and steep valleys to the canyons of difficulty their children will have to face.

Think of the determined dieter who, feeling incredibly motivated, purchases an athletic club membership with visions of total fitness and unprecedented health. For most of these weight warriors, within a few weeks or a couple of months, the pain sets in and motivation is sapped. *Seinfeld* and other more sedentary activities take priority replacing the will to endure and achieve the goal of total fitness.

Hundreds of thousands of married people become so excessively focused on career, reputation, money, and leisure that they neglect the more important responsibilities and commitments to their family lives. They forget the excitement of that wedding day, and they neglect the covenants made at the marriage alter. They neglect the vows which would enable them to make those goals a reality. Thousands of others choose involvement in deviant compulsions, which breed disrespect and heartache among those they love. They also rob themselves of the self-control required to live life responsibly and compassionately. Again, they are abandoning their original intent to find happiness in marriage and family. Children of these unions are brought up with shelter and some good times at best, but without any real direction and *Warnings* for their future. So many begin down the course to happiness but lack the endurance to stay the course.

Many of my own *Generation X* now wander through life without any real conviction or purpose, without direction, and pessimistic about their future. This is due in part to their parents' failure to build a very direct and specifically involved relationship with their children and then granting them many premature freedoms. This pessimism and lack of direction is the result of parents who have applied well-intentioned, but overbearing and unbending strictness without explanation, mercy, or compassion. This is because some parents' first attempts at real guidance come only after the adolescent is already engulfed in destructive behavior. They now mourn finding that their realm of influence has suffered the effects of atrophy as day-to-day instruction has been neglected.

For most of my *Generation X* friends there is no shortage of fun and adventure in their lives. Many of them though, will soon face a great famine of substance when they are forced to face up to the real responsibilities of life. Left uncorrected, they will remain adrift in this substantive famine for generations.

I once unwittingly experienced a similar famine first-hand. I am an above average runner, a very mediocre cyclist, and a sinking swimmer. So why not give a triathlon a try? That was my thinking three months before entering the Catalina Triathlon three years ago. I am young and in shape. No problem. I ran my heart out in preparation. I got a subscription to *Triathlete*. I rode miles to improve my cycling endurance. I swam lap after lap in the pool in an attempt to achieve even the slightest semblance of buoyancy. The day arrived, and I took my bike, goggles, cap, and *Powerbar* to the island.

The entire scene was exciting. I registered, and they marked my number, 103, on my shoulders and thighs with that neat black ink. I felt official. Very athletic. (Oh, how very naive.)

I was in the second wave of four to enter the water. We were to swim a little less than 1/2 a mile. A fairly short distance compared to more rigorous events. My goal was to stay in the middle of the pack. The first wave jumped at the sound of the gun, and the participants bounded down the beach and into the water. Splashing, kicking, just as it seemed when I watched the *Ironman* on ESPN. This was great!

Just standing amid the group in my first triathlon, cap secured, goggles in place and speedo snug gave me a feeling of accomplishment. Little did I realize that this actually was the highlight of the event for me. The gun sounded, I ran down to the water. I dove in and struggled to find a groove between the flailing arms of the competitors around me. Within the first 20-30 yards I knew I was in trouble. In all of my preparations I had never really taken into consideration the great difference between an 80-degree, 5' deep pool, and the 65-degree, choppy and bottomless ocean. I thought that all of my years surfing for hours upon hours would have automatically qualified me for the elements. Was I ever wrong! I found that I was unable to keep my face buried in the water for any length of time as I swam because the cool temperature caused me to lose my breath, I had to continually look up and gasp for air. Defeatedly, I resorted to the breaststroke and backstroke, while attempting to relax and find a rhythm. My muscles began to cramp, and I soon found myself at the very tail end of my group. I was sure that I had seen 60 year-old men and women in my group. I tried to put that hard fact out of my mind!

By the end of the swim I had been swiftly passed and brought up the rear, not of my group of swimmers, but of the third wave, who began their swim a full 10 minutes after us. Now I must say that I must have had some foresight as this was the first sporting event to which I decided to go alone, without family to cheer me on. Oh, what pain I spared us all!!

Legs like Jello, I walked up the beach to the changing area to prepare for the cycling. It was at this point that I realized I was all alone and that I could easily get on my bike and slip away into the hills of Catalina, find some cool shade and ease into slumber until my boat shoved off. And I really did contemplate that! But I knew I must press on and that when asked about my performance, I could always truthfully reply to my family fans back home that the swim just hadn't gone as well as planned. Period!

I remained in the middle of pack Number 3 for the remainder of the day, suffering much of the same preparation famine as I had in the swim. Let's just say that my long flat rides at home did little to prepare me for the five grueling laps around the hilly island, which to me resembled the heights of Mt. Kilamanjaro. During the run, my proud 5 1/2 minute, single mile time turned to dragging 10-12 minute-miles. I ran mile after mile through a course of hills and valleys I like to call the Swiss Alps. Finally, I crossed the finish line feeling thoroughly exhausted and so glad I was all alone!

After what felt like 72 hours since arriving on that quaint little isle, I finally boarded the cruiser. As we headed back to Long Beach, I sat next to the window stunned. I simply had had no idea. I felt good that I did not quit, but my athletic pride was squashed. I was no where near the athlete I thought I was. It took me about eight months, literally, before I could put my running shoes back on.

Looking back, it is easy to see why this event was so difficult for me. Not only had I trained very minimally, but I had never even attempted to combine all three events back-to-back in preparation. I only worked on each event separately. And so it is for many thousands of people who grow up without needed instruction. They find themselves in a world much more demanding than they ever imagined and suffer with much more fatigue and disappointment than they would have if they had had a better training experience. They come to find out that life is much like a triathlon with many intertwined and connected events. To find real success, there must be a period of real training and conditioning. Conditioning in as many events as possible develops personal endurance such that individuals can weather the combination of circumstance and opportunity that comes to everyone sooner or later.

Everyone is seeking happiness in life, yet so many end up in a place far removed from the happiness sought. Clouded perceptions of life make it very easy to wander down paths, which may be appealing but are not in any way beneficial. It is time we begin to teach the next generation specifically where true happiness is to be found. We must be certain that the next generation understands it is a wonderful thing to seek success in education and career. It is noble to aspire to the top of their field and become as successful as they believe they can be. It is good to seek adventure, travel the world and experience many exciting moments in life. It is good to enjoy music, fashion, art, and entertainment. However, they must also be taught that these alone will not bring the success and satisfaction they are seeking in life. They must understand that all of these things are supplements to the deeper, more lasting success and joy which comes from service to others, responsibility for self, honor to marriage vows, time and patience with children, kindness to others, and integrity.

Ask any of the great achievers in life what is important. Ask the movie star whose fame has dimmed, the athlete whose time has passed, the retired CEO, a past political giant, or a renown professor. Most will agree that after the fanfare and the hoopla pass, the only happiness that truly endures is that which is derived from the ever-important principles of service, integrity and honor to faith and family.

Stuart E. Rosenberg expresses it well when he writes, "Despite all new inventions and modern designs, fads, and fetishes; no one has yet invented, or will ever invent, a satisfying substitute for one's own family."

After the lights go down, most agree there is no greater joy and no greater achievement than to attain love and happiness at home and to pass that formula on to the children they love.

With all of his fame and recognition, our beloved President Abraham Lincoln had this to say concerning his success, "All that I am and all that I hope to be I owe to my angel mother. Blessings on her memory."

My generation and the next must come to know these truths about their own faith and responsibility to family. They will begin a course that they believe will lead them to happiness with or without us. And they can only learn from sad experience or careful warning that many of the pathways that at first appear to lead to happiness only lead to destinations of disappointment. If they have no clear goals to look toward, they will go with whatever seems right, and they will eventually get exactly what they seek, good or bad, as so stated in the poem at the beginning of this chapter, "... if dogged and grim you beseech and beset it, you'll get it!"

I am convinced that simple and consistent teachings will serve to provide valuable safety nets and lifelines for our young ones to rely on. Having gone before them, we can help many more of them attain success in the milestone events of life. They will experience the joys of raising their own families, rather than repeating the struggles of the broken homes they may have come from. They will better cope with the trials and sorrows of life, which they will unavoidably face. They will learn to admit their errors and will work to overcome their imperfections. They will finally come to know for themselves and pass on to the next generation that the truly great achievements and joy in their lives have little to do with fortune or fame, but everything to do with faith, friendship, and family.

CHAPTER 4:

Fair Warning

If we work marble it will perish; if we work upon brass, time will efface it; if we rear temples, they will crumble into dust; but if we work upon immortal minds and instill into them just principles, we are then engraving upon tablets which no time will efface, but will brighten to all eternity.

- Author unknown

You have moved to the mountains. You have built your dream home on the bank of a beautiful, flowing river. One Saturday afternoon you decide to head up that familiar trail to your favorite fishing hole. The oft traveled path bends through the canyon floor for about one mile before gradually ascending the canyon wall to the top of the dam. There you find your small motor boat and shove off towards your secluded cove for an afternoon of fishing.

Unfortunately, today did not produce the desired catch. Two solid days of torrential rains and run-off created a lake of dark and unsettled murkiness. The lake is swollen to capacity, nearly 50 feet higher than any time during the last five years. The overflow of debris and sediment dashed all hopes of bringing dinner home.

Four hours later it is evening, and you begin the descent into the valley walking adjacent to the dam itself. The water rushes from the opposite end of the dam and into the river. It fills your ears as its violent gushing echoes through the canyon. Louder and faster than ever before.

As you reach the base of the dam and begin to head down the river bed path through the trees towards home, a loud snapping, crackling sound from above startles you. Shielding your head, you crouch and quickly look up and behind you. It is dark, and you can scarcely make out the top of the dam. As you gaze up towards the structure's crest, you faintly hear what seems to be rocks bouncing off the face of the dam and plunging into the water beside you.

Another cracking burst. More falling debris. All at once, terror strikes your heart, and you feel your blood run cold as you realize what is happening. This dam is about to give way! You drop everything and begin to sprint through the woods towards your home. Your mind is racing. Ten minutes? One hour? How much time will we have to flee this canyon? Can I possibly make it in time?

Halfway to your home and family, you come to a grinding halt. The porch light of your only neighbor, who is situated on the opposite bank, beams into your wide eyes. They have no idea. Probably eating dinner and enjoying the evening together. Heart racing, you know you must sacrifice another five minutes to head deeper into the woods and backtrack a bit to the entrance of one of two bridges in the canyon. The river is now swelling, and you do what you know you must despite your great anxiety for the safety of your own family. You warn your neighbor. You save their lives.

Twenty minutes later you and your family stand next to your neighbors safe and dry, 10 miles downstream and on high ground. The valley is washed out, and both homes are gone. Yet, you have never felt more grateful. You have never felt better.

It is my belief that such a hero lies within nearly all of us. Most of us are willing to help out in an emergency situation if we have any ability to do so. Most people will jump into action during a sudden life or death situation when no one else is there to help, even if it requires the sacrifice of their own safety. Every day people across the country pull victims from burning homes, help out at car wrecks, search for missing persons, and warn their friends and neighbors when disaster is coming.

We should be proud of our efforts and teamwork in these crisis situations. Organizations jump into action to assist victims of natural disasters. Counselors swarm upon groups and individuals who have suffered at the hands of criminals. Drug rehab programs throughout the country assist those who have ruined their lives with drug and alcohol abuse. Hotlines comfort the heavy hearts of those who are physically and sexually abused. I wonder, how many of these crisis situations might have been prevented? What if we were as effective in the area of prevention as we are in the event of crisis?

Sure, there are many events that cannot be easily foreseen. A car wreck. A natural disaster. A criminal act. And we do a pretty good job preparing for these unexpected, unforeseen events. We spend a few years pushing seat belt use. We have many good neighborhood crime watch programs. Smoke alarms and fire extinguishers are found in every supply store. We put up secure fences around the pool. We have taken some preventative measures, but most of us still have that feeling that it won't happen to us, and do not prepare as carefully as we could.

For instance, a couple of years ago I purchased two, 50-gallon drums to store water in in case of an earthquake or some other natural disaster. Very wise planning, don't you think? (Did you see the mad dash for water during the 1995 Northridge, CA quake? Some store owners were later convicted of severe price gouging amid the mad demand for such necessities.) Yet, the drums in my garage remain empty. In over two years I have not taken 10 minutes out of my day to rinse them out, add some purifying solution, and run the hose into them. I park next to them every time I pull into the garage and think about filling them on a regular basis and simply continue to put it off.

I find it highly ironic that through all of our experience as a country, we largely neglect to warn and fail to act heroically in the moments that matter most and over which we have the most control and foresight. With a little luck, the family who never wears seat belts, bicycle helmets, or installs fire alarms may never meet injury or disaster. However, the person who does not prepare for or define some direction in day-to-day living definitely suffers a personal disaster and we all know this. We all know by now that alcohol and drugs can ruin a person's life. They can lead to violence, theft, drunk driving, loss of employment, loss of family, etc. We all know that stealing and dishonesty can lead to years in jail, further crimes, and an overall loss of trust. We know that inappropriate flirtation, and giving in to sexual impulses and suggestions can lead to infidelity that can crush a family. We know that young kids are heavily influenced by what they see around them and at the same time are very ignorant about real life.

Yet, parents give their young children sips of beer at family picnics for a laugh. They instill a level of excitement at turning 21 and being able to drink legally. Why such excitement and anticipation when the risks are so high? Is drinking alcohol really so important that we should overlook the risks just to satisfy the norm? Parents smoke in front of their children for years. They go to the movies and buy tickets at the 12 year-old price for and in front of their 14 year-old child. They call in sick to work when they are actually just sick of work. They cheat on each other. They yell at each other. They teach their kids to do exactly as they do. They epitomize the oft-repeated phrase, "Your actions speak so loudly, I can hardly hear what you're saying!"

The beloved Billy Graham observed, "We are preoccupied with material things. Our supreme god is technology; our goddess is sex. Most of us are more interested in getting to the moon than in getting to heaven, more concerned about conquering space than about conquering ourselves. We are more dedicated to material security than to inner purity. We give much more thought to what we wear, what we eat, what we drink and what we can do to relax than we give to what we are."

Instead of setting the example themselves, these parents think, hope or assume that their kids will somehow still do better than they have done. Maybe they think their children will figure it out as they go along. It is as if the man in the canyon, in his hurried and excited attempt to flee the oncoming disaster, decides to forego crossing the bridge to warn his neighbor because he figures his neighbor will hear the water rushing through his yard and that will be warning enough. Maybe he will have enough time to get away!

Brett Easton Ellis recently wrote in an article featured in *George Magazine*, "It would be easy to be glib and condescending about the topic of kids in America, but things have changed drastically in the last 20 years, to the point where one can only really chuckle in grim disbelief. Cheating on exams? Smoking cigarettes? Shoplifting? You wish. Murder, rape, robbery, vandalism: the overwhelming majority of these crimes are committed by people under 25, and the rate is escalating rapidly."

He continues, "Given that the generation who raised this group of kids was so disconnected, so embroiled in its own narcissism, who can blame the kids themselves? We get the kids we deserve. And when your formative years are so sketchy, and you live in a world where drugs are as available as soda, and sex will kill you if it's not planned carefully; a world where divorce reigns; where your fear of violence is so paralyzing your classmates carry box cutters and guns to school; and then you pile on top of this world the usual set of adolescent anxieties, is it any wonder that kids either turn into computer geeks alienated from actual experience or retreat into the solidarity of urban gang life? What did we expect the outcome to be? Eddie Haskell?"

In the same article, Melissa Rossi quotes James Allen Fox, Dean of Criminal Justice at Boston's Northeastern University who said, "We are facing a potential blood bath of teenage violence in years ahead that will be so bad, we'll look back at the 1990s and say those were the good old days."

She further quotes Pulitzer Prize winning author Edward Humes, whose recent book, *No Matter How Loud I Shout*, documents a year in the LA juvenile court. He says, "We have an army forming on the horizon. It's going to invade in the next 10-15 years, and we are not doing anything to defend ourselves."

Are we really defending ourselves? I think Mr. Humes has a point. We must more effectively defend ourselves. Unless we are willing to tackle these problems head-on with real, sustained effort family by family across America, we will find ourselves trapped as the pathetic passengers on a plane over which they have no control are, illustrated in the following story I heard told by James B. Whitesides.

While en route, a small plane suddenly jolts and startles all aboard. Immediately the pilot tells the group that one engine has failed, but that everything is under control, and they will land safely within 30 minutes. Most ease back comfortably into their chairs. Again, the violent jarring is repeated. Quickly the pilot affirms that another engine has been lost, but not to fear, the aircraft is still under control and will land shortly. Now an overall tension permeates the entire plane. Another bout of sputtering and a third engine fails. Now most aboard begin to rustle and some cry out in wonder and fear. At this point both pilots emerge from the cockpit wearing parachute packs! The pilot raises his hand to get their attention. All are waiting for his instructions, and he says, "Now don't any of you worry! We are going for help!" A hatch is quickly opened, and the two bail out together.

We just may find ourselves in such a position of powerlessness in the years to come. In our society, the war against drugs, the increasing violence, and other related problems seem to me to have been handled in the way many are forced to pay bills: from week to week. Many are so behind financially that as money comes in it is immediately spent on past-due bills. Accumulated unnecessary debt is at the point that every cent of income is already spoken for and that family never finds a break in the payment cycle, which would allow them to put something substantial aside for themselves. They have virtually lost their ability to shore up savings as protection for a rainy day. Yet, they remain unwilling to change their lifestyle and make the sacrifice of giving up certain *things* enabling them to catch up and to save for their financial future.

The tide of trouble for our youth is rising so quickly that we spend put most of our effort into things like teaching kids how to wear a condom after they have already begun having sex. The hopes of teaching abstinence to such kids is now greatly diminished. And we are so busy fighting the overwhelming influx of illegal drugs that we can do little to influence the demand.

For every one of my friends who came away from the teen years with an addiction to drugs or alcohol, I remember parents who never addressed my friends' problems until they were out of control and virtually beyond reach. These are the same parents who drove them to parties in the seventh grade, assuming they were playing pin the tail on the donkey and that other parents were running the night's activities. Actually, the parents weren't even home, and they had left plenty of liquor around the house, while they had gone away for the weekend.

We are running a huge deficit in our effort to slow the growth of decadence. We hope to catch up with the problems now looming before us, but never give enough careful attention to the next generation. It is the next generation that can effectively and naturally slow the speed of social decay. This will only occur when a far more Americans are willing to make sacrifices of time and personal convenience necessary to raise a group of young adults who find better things to do than waste away in the now.

In the big picture of life, we only have a few years to be at home and learn from our parents or guardians. I think I deserved and received the best possible training while I was at home. Looking back, overall I had fantastic experience. I was actually taught specifics about life and what to expect when I got out there. I am grateful that my parents did not have a limited view of successful parenting.

What I mean is that most of my friends had one of two types of parents. The first and most ineffective type were the ones who let their kids experience practically anything. They had no objection to certain rowdy friends and gave virtually no direction or real care whatsoever. Most of the other kids saw these parents as *totally cool!*

And then there were the more strict parents who emphasized homework, sports, cheerleading, and other activities. These felt that if their child was active in sports and social activities, received good grades and was accepted into a college, they had succeeded in raising a stellar child. Everything looks good on paper. These children were seen as on their way to a successful future. Most likely, they would land a good job and end up making a solid income.

Now we all know the probable result of the kids raised by the first type of parents. But what about those raised by the second type? Most would agree that they did succeed because their child pulled down good grades and went off to college. Furthermore, these offspring have a very good chance of landing good jobs. But have those accomplishments alone really secured success for those kids? Everything looks good, but is it? What did they actually teach their kids? Did they cheat in school? Do they go to college and sleep around and cheat on boyfriends and girlfriends? Do they drink themselves into oblivion once they get there? Do they talk down to and about those with whom they associate? Is it possible that many of these kids are only postponing personal troubles? In their pursuit of knowledge, have they been exposed to or received any real wisdom from their parents?

Look at the hundreds of thousands of individuals who have secured a solid education and gone on to be productive members of society but still suffer through heart-wrenching divorces, even multiple divorces. What of the thousands in corporate America who sustain vicious addictions to alcohol, drugs, sex and power? What of the thousands who are involved in corporate crime, sexual harassment, affairs in the workplace, and racism? What of the thousands who make solid, six-figure incomes as a result of their collegiate success, but have no relationship with their children and treat their spouses as secondary to money and prestige?

Don't our children deserve *Fair Warning* about these long-term obstacles? Don't they deserve parents who are willing to warn them and plead with them to avoid the mistakes they have made and to avoid the many pitfalls only those experienced in life can reveal? Don't they deserve to have parents who are concerned with their children's ability to sustain the good life throughout their lives and not just until college graduation? I will be forever indebted to my parents who warned me and counseled me concerning those things, which would or could effect me many years down the road if I did not begin to understand the long-term effects of my youthful decisions and habits. I am indebted to my parents who encouraged education, sports, and social activities as supplements to the mosaic of my life. As a means to a much greater end, which I have yet to completely experience.

I consider myself one who certainly would have wandered down roads to terrible destinations if it hadn't been for the extra efforts made by my parents. I had every opportunity to do wrong. At times while growing up I displayed the common teenage tendencies of argumentativeness, laziness, and other typical youthful improprieties. On occasion, however, I was confronted with opportunities to be involved in more dangerous and rebellious activities. But in the midst of all of this, I had something within me, which nearly all of my friends did not. I had clear-cut knowledge of right and wrong which resulted in a healthy conscience. If I crossed certain barriers I felt the guilt. The more serious the compromise, the more acute the guilt became. (And so it is to this day) I could not deny that I was veering off-course. Because of this knowledge of right and wrong I had no excuses. I knew I had to change. My parents had already warned me. They had not threatened me. They did not shelter me in an overbearing manner. They were not perfect and made their fair share of mistakes, but they always honored their responsibility to explain right and wrong in every situation they knew was a threat to my future. They did their very best to live as they taught. They admitted their faults. They regularly exhibited and expressed their love. They built the necessary fences around my life to protect me, and then left me the freedom to choose my course. The result? Rebellious phases were always short-lived, while my friends had no reason to stop and consider changing their course. Most of them still have not.

And for my siblings? Chris, four years ahead of me, probably exhibited a bit more of the common youthful baggage such as argumentation, etc. However, he experimented very little, if at all, with the more life-threatening temptations that were ever before him. He lives well within the wise boundaries our parents originally established and now, under the influence of his wonderful wife, Conni, is raising an even greater family than ours had been.

Greg, four years ahead of Chris, spent 15 years of his life off and on involved in the use of illicit drugs and a host of other related indulgences I won't bother listing. A parental failure? Hardly. Greg has made it back to life. Married to a truly great and admirable woman, Rozeanne, they have five beautiful children and are raising them fantastically. Had it not been for the principles instilled years earlier, doubtless he would have gone on to a life of crime, prison and misery. He is an example of one who, without direction, would have been another sad statistic of drug use, violence, and homelessness. In the end, what he learned years ago at home prevailed and he now looks to our parents with inexplicable gratitude.

Our parents, while tending to their own lives and sacrificing much, so very much along the way, will be forever honored by their three sons and their families for making the extra effort to build a fence of safety and wisdom around them.

Carefully consider the words of the Englishman, Joseph Malins who many years ago wrote this poem entitled *A Fence or an Ambulance* based on the adage "An ounce of prevention is better than a pound of cure."

'Twas a dangerous cliff, as they freely confessed,
Though to walk near its crest was so pleasant;
But over its terrible edge there had slipped
A duke and full many a peasant.
So the people said something would have to be done,
But their projects did not at all tally;
Some said, "Put a fence around the edge of the cliff,"
Some, "An ambulance down in the valley."

But the cry for the ambulance carried the day,
For it spread through the neighboring city;
A fence may be useful or not it is true,
But each heart became brimful of pity
For those who slipped over that dangerous cliff;
And the dwellers in highway and alley
Gave pounds or gave pence, not to put up a fence,
But an ambulance down in the valley.

"For the cliff is alright, if you're careful," they said,
"And, if folks even slip or are dropping,
It isn't the slipping that hurts them so much,
As the shock down below when they're stopping."
So day after day, as these mishaps occurred,
Quick forth would these rescuers sally
To pick up the victims who fell off the cliff,
With the ambulance down in the valley.

Then an old sage remarked: "It's a marvel to me
That people give far more attention
To repairing results than to stopping the cause,
When they'd much better aim at prevention,
Let us stop at its source all this mischief," cried he,

"Come, neighbors and friends, let us rally;
If the cliff we will fence we might almost dispense
With the ambulance down in the valley."

"Oh, he's a fanatic," the others rejoined,
"Dispense with the ambulance? Never!
He'd dispense with all charities, too, if he could;
No! No! we'll support them forever.
Aren't we picking up folks just as fast as they fall?
And shall this man dictate to us? Shall he?
Why should people of sense stop to put up a fence,
While the ambulance works down in the valley?"

But a sensible few, who are practical too,
Will not bear with such nonsense much longer;
They believe that prevention is better than cure,
And their party will soon be the stronger.
Encourage them then, with your purse, voice, and pen,
And while other philanthropists dally,
They will scorn all pretense and put up a stout fence
On a cliff that hangs over the valley.

Better guide well the young than reclaim them when old,
For the voice of true wisdom is calling,
"To rescue the fallen is good, but 'tis best
To prevent other people from falling."
Better close up the source of temptation and crime
Than deliver from dungeon and galley;
Better put a strong fence round the top of the cliff
Than an ambulance down in the valley.

(*The Best Loved Poems of the American People* [New York: Doubleday, 1936],pp.273-274.)

It is true that even as we build these fences for our families, there will be some who will climb over them. Despite our
very best efforts, there will be children we work so diligently
to preserve who will go their own way despite our efforts.
These will be the minority. And each diligent parent who has
one of those determined to learn the hard way will at least be
able to feel satisfied that they did all they could, thereby
avoiding the deep regret that accompanies parental neglect.
And for those few determined to choose dangerous paths,
there will be thousands upon thousands more who easily
could do likewise, but will be saved from a life of directionless
agony because of the extra efforts and *Fair Warnings* they
receive from their parents.

Individually, may we be mindful of the words of Marcus
Aurelius, who writes, "A wrongdoer is often a man who has
left something undone, not always that he has done something wrong."

Collectively, may we be mindful of these words of wisdom
from an unknown author who wrote, "A society that permits
anything, will eventually lose everything."

In our struggle to help our youth acquire knowledge we
must remember not to neglect the more significant attainment
of wisdom. Knowledge is wonderful and absolutely necessary, it
is the ever-important acquiring of the facts of history, science,
technology, arts, religion, and politics. Wisdom though, is the
more meaningful acquisition of the ability to reason, decipher,
listen, and love coupled with the ability to apply learning and
experience to negotiating, maintaining self-control, extending
compassion and understanding, and serving unselfishly. We
cannot feel secure raising bright and knowledgeable youth who
are without the needful exposure to wisdom which finally leads
to the possession of wisdom.

Dwight D. Eisenhower said, "A man with knowledge and great moral principles is a great man; but a man with knowledge and no moral principles is only a clever devil."

This point is also put well by John Ruskin who said, "Education does not mean teaching people to know what they do not know; it means teaching them to behave as they do not behave."

Henry Ford added his insight, "An educated man is not one whose memory is trained to carry a few dates in history. He is one who can accomplish things. A man who cannot think is not an educated man however many college degrees he may have acquired. Thinking is the hardest work anyone can do, which is probably the reason why we have so few thinkers."

As we attempt to instill wisdom, this invaluable tool for life, we can raise a generation that will not leave things undone. They will create a society wise enough to put an end to the permission of all things working to diminish a structured society as we know it. We will have given them this *Fair Warning* of which I speak and will have taught them much more than just how to get into a fine school, but how to become a fine person and how to think rationally and logically as well. We will have crossed the bridge of personal sacrifice in order to warn them of the oncoming floods they will face in their lives.

In the first four chapters I have attempted to establish a few important points and make certain clarifications before discussing specific areas wherein lie the roots of eventual failings or the bedrock foundation necessary for lifelong achievement.

First, we are in urgent need of strong families led by great parents in today's society. It is clear that if the quality and stability of family life does not improve within the coming years, we will witness the growth of insurmountable societal dilemmas.

Second, as parents we possess more power and opportunity to

change and ultimately save this country than any other individual or organization. Our children will eventually control the institutions which set agendas and create laws, just as the children of the Sixties, the Boomers, have a stronghold on these institutions today.

Second, we need to evaluate closely and be willing to sacrifice the amount of time and effort we spend in pursuit of our social, occupational, and financial goals, which we expect will bring joy and fulfillment. We must realize that after all is said and done, there is no greater fulfillment than that of a successful home and family.

Third, we know about life's dangers. We owe it to the children we have accepted stewardship over to extend to them the *Fair Warnings* which will serve to protect and benefit their futures.

In the following chapters we will look at some of the areas to which these *Fair Warnings* must be extended. This is requisite for the upcoming generation to move ahead and avoid the perpetuation of what we now know the stereotypical *Generation X* to be. I will share some facts, some real-life personal experiences, and some experiences of others from my generation in an attempt to emphasize and shed new light on many things of which we are all very much aware but may be leaving undone.

Some of what I have to say in the following chapters concerning the media, honesty, friendships, attitudes, alcohol, sex, service, etc. may at times seem hard to swallow. Some may feel that there is too much influence out there and many of my suggestions are too strict or unrealistic. To those who feel it can't be done, that kids just will not live without experiencing certain things, I suggest that they underestimate the ability of youth to make good choices if they have the right amount of direction and loving encouragement.

I hope I can cut through much of the psycho-babble and get

to the heart of things. That we will love our kids to success by teaching, counseling, spending more time, showing more affection, building needed fences, and setting better examples. That we will no longer stand aside and wait for an unexplained upswing in society, rather, we begin now through a collective effort to positively force a change in our society. That we can jump in with both feet, knowing mistakes will be made and learning from them along the way.

Mark Twain once said, "The man walking down the street carrying a cat by the tail is gaining at least ten times as much experience as the man who is just standing there watching him."

We must do all in our power paying whatever painful price, sacrificing more, and obtaining a clearer perspective to avoid the inevitable fate of our society outlined by Laurence M. Gould who said, "I do not believe that the greatest threat to our future is from bombs or guided missiles. I don't think our civilization will die that way. I think it will die when we no longer care. Arnold Toynbee has pointed out that, 'nineteen or twenty civilizations have died from within and not by conquest from without.' There were no bands playing and flags waving when these civilizations decayed. It happened slowly, in the quiet and the dark when no one was aware."

THREE

THE FAIR WARNINGS

CHAPTER 5:

Friends, Acquaintances and Their Influence

Every boy, in his heart, would rather steal second base than an automobile.

- Midwest City Bulletin

How many of your high school and college friends and acquaintances do you still keep in touch with today? How many of them do you still send holiday greeting cards to? How many of them would you call on the phone in a time of crisis? One? Three, five, or possibly six? The fact is, we lose touch with most of them, and those we do keep in touch with have little influence over us at this point. We grow apart as we make our way through life. We make new friends in our chosen professional fields and in our new cities and towns.

Dig up an old yearbook. How many friends have you completely forgotten? Yet these were the people with whom you spent the majority of your time while growing up. You spent time with them in class, sports, cheerleading, recreation, parties, and practically every waking moment away from home. You spent hour upon hour with these people. These friends, whether many or only a select few, were unquestionably some of the most significant and powerful influences in your life. You heard the way they talked, and you talked like them. You saw the way they reacted and responded to countless situations, and you acted like them. You watched them make serious decisions about drinking, drugs, and sex; and you usually did what they did. You heard what they said about everyone else, and you said it too. Did they influence you for good or ill? In most cases, upon serious reflection, the majority of school time friends and acquaintances did very little to help you become a better person. They usually wanted you to try all of the *fun* stuff like, drinking, ditching class, gossiping, and staying out all night with them. They wanted you to join them in every sort of experiment and mischief. They contributed to the overall *peer pressure* of young life. I believe you will probably recall only a select few whom you say had an overall positive and constructive influence on you.

Consider some of the results of a survey, which I distributed to 200, 18-30 year-old college students:

Who or what was your most negative influence while growing up?

    65% indicate that friends were their greatest negative influence.

    20% indicate that parents or family members were their most negative influence.

    15% indicate that TV and other miscellaneous sources were their most negative influence.

Who or what was your most positive influence while growing up?

    58% state that their parents were their most positive influence.

    22% state that their friends and siblings were their most positive influence.

    20% state that religion and other miscellaneous sources were their most positive influence.

Has school or government ever influenced you to avoid sex and drugs?

    82% No

    18% Yes

Were you ever taught how or why you should choose good, positive friends to hang out with?

    62% No

    38% Yes

It is interesting to note that 65% of those surveyed admit that their friends, the ones they loved to spend time with for all those years, were actually the most negative influence. Also, after all the rebellion and stress they gave their parents for enforcing all of their *dos* and *don'ts*, the truth finally comes home to roost. Parents were, after all, the most positive influence on 58% of the participants. The survey also suggests that schools and government have little effect instilling moral behavior in young people, as 82% say they were not influenced by either school systems or the government to avoid detrimental behavior. In my opinion, the most significant statistic is that only 38% of these young adults ever remember any instruction or guidance from their parents concerning their selection of friends. I think it is interesting to note, schools do not significantly influence our kids morally, parents have the greatest positive influence, while friends have the least.

A good friend of mine might have avoided a terrible situation had he received a little parental counsel concerning his choice in company.

We'll call him Alex Ruiz. He played Roadrunner football with me in the sixth grade. We were both ridiculously tiny defensive backs who shared the same cornerback position. On occasion his mom would drive us to the beach so we could surf all day together. She always seemed like a very *cool* mom. His uncle was a bass player for a world-renowned rock band and Alex would often tell me about hanging out backstage whenever they played in the area.

As we entered the big league, junior high of course, we went our separate ways. We lived in different attendance areas, so he went off to one school, and I headed to another. It was a few years before I ran into Alex again, we were both incredibly cool freshmen in high school. Although, to me he was a little cooler than I at this point because he had actually grown to an acceptable height. I still hovered merely inches from the earth, slightly bigger than a bread box.

We ran into each other at a Friday night high school football game. Immediately I noticed a dramatic change in my old friend. His head was now shaved nearly bald, and he wore a plain white T-shirt and jeans with absurdly large military boots, which laced up just two inches below his kneecaps. It was obvious he was not nearly as interested in seeing me again as I was seeing him. In our brief conversation, he mentioned he was moving to Colorado soon. Then he quickly walked off with a similarly dressed friend. I thought very little of the meeting.

As I opened my locker between classes during the first semester of my sophomore year, my friend, Danny Carlson, walked up and without saying a word handed me the latest edition of *Time Magazine*. The cover featured mug shots of four teenagers under bold headline which read, "AMERICA'S MOST WANTED TEENS." In the bottom right corner was a picture of my old friend, Alex Ruiz, head shaven, stoney-faced with blemishes. In stunned amazement I turned to the article and read how Alex was wanted for murder in Denver, Colorado. As a member of a racist skinhead group, he and two others had lain in-wait for a homosexual hairdresser as he closed up his salon. As the hairdresser left the salon, he was brutally beaten by the three young men, set aflame and then dumped into a nearby body of water.

I can't help wondering what his fate might have been if we had gone to the same schools. I also wonder what concern if any was shown by his mother when she noticed the obvious signs of change: the clothing, his new look and the less than social friends. How late was he out each night and with whom? Were there any rules? Had she been enforcing guidelines over the years? Perhaps this would have helped her maintain rules for her teen.

A story is told of an independent, little, nine year-old boy who one day announced to his mother and father one night at the dinner table, "I am running away from home tomorrow. Who is going to drive me?" Children are not born bad. They are innocent and powerless to undertake even the smallest of tasks without help. For many years they are forced by their own limitations to learn from and be guided by their parents Due to this awesome responsibility, it is incumbent upon us, as parents, to keep our children involved in wholesome and productive activities and know where they go and with whom.

We are not talking about paranoid shelter here. We are talking about reasonable, loving guidance. Everyone on this earth will have associations with so-called *bad influences*. In fact, I suggest that most parents would be absolutely shocked to see all of the compromising individuals and situations their children are subjected to on a regular basis, starting at a very young age and in the most unexpected places. As little children, they all meet the *friend* who teaches them their first swear words, shows them their first dirty picture, teaches them how to hold a cigarette, persuades them to steal a pack of gum, encourages them to pick a fight, and so on. It occurs on the playground, in friends' homes, in the classroom, at Sunday School, at Little League games, and at the neighborhood park.

We all recognize that our kids inevitably will be exposed to these people and these situations probably sooner rather than later. It is a necessary part of life to meet these individuals and situations head on. We all must learn to deal with the different types of people and situations that we face in life. It would do no good to try and completely shelter our children from the *world*. This process of exposure builds character and social maturity if handled correctly. Parents must see that their children are not unnecessarily over-exposed. Children cannot be allowed to spend countless hours of unsupervised, idle time with those shady kids of whom we know all the horror stories or know nothing about at all. They must be supervised so they can find the balance between minimal exposure and detrimental over-exposure. It would be impossible, unhealthy, and unwise to simply attempt to shield our children from everyone who might persuade them to do wrong. They must have the opportunity to exercise their own freedom of choice and fall down occasionally, then with your help pick themselves up and try again.

Case in point: During my fourteenth year, I finally received the package I had been waiting for over eight weeks to arrive. My eyes fixed on the only word which mattered in the entire letter, "Congratulations!" I was going to Mexico, and I was elated!

I was one of 14 teenagers selected to represent the United States in a foreign exchange, freestyle and Greco-Roman wrestling tournament in Mexico City. I qualified after competing in a series of tournaments during the 1986 spring wrestling season in Southern California. I would represent my country in the notoriously intimidating 88-pound weight class.

All of the necessary legal and organizational arrangements were made and the time had finally come. We spent six days in Mexico City until the end of the tournament. We then flew to Cancun for an additional five days of sight-seeing and relaxing in the sun. All appeared well and good, and I am sure my parents were just as excited to send me as I was to go.

When we arrived at the hotel, we were given maps of the area by our three coaches. This was virtually the last time I saw those men. We were told when to be here or there, then were left completely on our own from that point on. We saw our vacationing coaches only at the tournament sight, on one or two planned tours and at the airport. Surely, this amount of free reign had not been spelled out in the original itinerary. The next 11 days proved to be the most eye-opening, innocence-shattering experience of my life.

Pete, 17 years-old, born and raised in Los Angeles, was the only one who spoke Spanish. He became the team's night life leader.

"Taxi!" He yelled out. It was about 8:00 PM and all 14 of us piled into two taxi cabs. I squeezed into the front seat next to Pete. "Donde?" asked the old man. "Red light district," came the excited reply.

"Red light district." I thought about those words. I had heard that phrase somewhere before. I couldn't recall what it meant exactly though. An arcade? Maybe a laser show? I wasn't sure. Everyone seemed really excited. I was having a lot of fun.

We pulled off the main street and headed down a dark alley. We parked next to a trash bin, and the taxi cab driver gave what I sensed were some sort of specific instructions. Everyone was quiet and Pete leaned back and said, "Now all of you just shut up, and follow me. Don't make any noise." Then he looked over at me and said, "Chavez, you stay here with Ramsey, we'll be back in about an hour." They all left including the taxi drivers.

There we were, Ramsey (our destructive 105-pounder) and me, (88 pounds of prowess) in a dark alley somewhere in the middle of Mexico City. We still weren't sure what kind of red light game they were playing up there; we only knew that we were scared out of our wits as we sat there, alone, slouched down in the back seat of the cab.

After watching two or three men stumble down the alley past us, we decided it was time to get out of there. When the coast was clear, we scrambled down the littered alley, around a large building and up five flights of steel stairs that had no railing and were lit with a red bulb at each landing. The stairway ended, and we were looking down a dark hallway that led to a large, red, smoke filled room. As we walked down the hall and into the room, we saw all of our teammates sitting at a table in the corner laughing and drinking. The room was filled with the most vile women I had ever seen, all clad in cheap lingerie, strutting around the room and hanging on the shoulders of some of the men. All at once I knew exactly what the red light district was, and I could hardly believe I was there.

After about an hour of watching my team drink each other under the table, Pete, our brave leader, suddenly appeared strolling toward us from a dark corridor. He acted as if he had accomplished something worthwhile with his little prostitute on his arm, and a sneaky smirk on his face. None of the other guys had the money required for the *purchase* if you will, so we all got up to leave. At that point the proprietor of the brothel pulled out a large pistol, bellowed a loud, rolling Spanish curse and stood in front of the only exit. Ramsey and I began to cry like babies.

The less-than-stellar business man wanted payment for the two bottles of tequila he had originally offered as a gift. He was demanding the special "Americano" price of just $50 per bottle. We had only $30 among us. I really thought I would be killed right there, just 14 years old, in the middle of a house-of-prostitution, over an unpaid liquor bill.

Our taxi cab driver acted as our mediator and continued to point towards Ramsey and me as we wept for our lives in an attempt to solicit sympathy from this corrupt man. After over 30 minutes of negotiations, he finally relented taking all of our money and giving a quick wave of his gun as the signal for us to get out. We were out the door, down the stairs, and dove head first into the two cabs at lightning speed.

We made it back to the hotel that night and every night thereafter by what seemed like the skin of our teeth. During the week I heard some of the guys bragging about the results of their sex contest: who could have the most sex before going home. I witnessed the fights, the drunken vomiting, and the overall mayhem that went on every night of the trip. Finally, I arrived home with a tanned body, two shiny tournament medals, and a whole new perspective.

It would be many years before I told my mom and dad about the details of that trip. They had no idea we had been left to ourselves in such a way. Since there were no red flags to indicate the total lack of supervision that would justify keeping me home, I had been allowed to go and reap the rewards of my efforts and be trusted.

I share this experience to point out the fact that there will be scores of compromising events and people who will enter the lives of your kids, while they are away from your immediate influence. These events will arise even after you have done all in your power to ensure they are out of harms way as my parents did before this trip. Once on their own; all they will have to direct them is their conscience, and what they learned about right and wrong at home. Why then, would you not monitor and influence the time and whereabouts spent with certain friends? Why not make an extra effort to get to know your children's friends? Find out for yourself if they are a good or bad influence on your child. Why not teach your children the value of choosing beneficial friends in an attempt to limit the number of compromising situations they will have to deal with and risk falling into?

Pete obviously had not been given a whole lot of guidance in his life. He was like a loose cannon when given the opportunity to choose for himself. He fit the classic profile of the leader of the group who always has that *bright* idea, which was actually nothing but trouble. It was as if he had waited his whole life to be out on his own and experience the world's darkest corners.

In retrospect, I recognize that most of the other guys were experiencing many of these temptations for the first time themselves. Ramsey avoided involvement only because he latched on to me. Then he was able to avoid the pressures of experiencing things he was so obviously afraid of at 14 years-old. I wonder if he had another friend to help him in a year or so when the next opportunity presented itself?

Over the years I have watched a few of these same guys, including Pete, remain close friends, wrestle on the same college team and room together. I wonder if they ever did clean up their acts? Keeping each other as constant company, their odds of mellowing are probably very low, their chances of continuing their dangerous mischief certainly remain high.

Ex-con Harold Morris has spent nearly 20 years warning young people to avoid the snares that nearly destroyed his life. In his well-circulated video presentation, *Twice Pardoned*, Harold talks about the perilous effects of peer pressure and how little mistakes can have big consequences.

As a young man, Harold was an All-American athlete with many scholarships available to him. He relates his experience of choosing to run with the wrong crowd, and how that choice altered his life forever. After making new friends at a night club, Harold found himself behind the wheel of the getaway car after his two new associates robbed a store and fatally shot the attendant. He had no prior knowledge of their plans to commit these crimes. Within one year, Harold was arrested and given two life sentences for armed robbery and murder. This was accomplished with the help of sworn testimony against him from the two *friends* who had actually committed the crimes themselves.

He spent over 10 years behind bars that ended when he received a miraculous pardon. Over the years since his release, Harold has talked to thousands of young people about his experience. When referring to his false imprisonment, he tells them, "Now don't you feel sorry for me! I consorted with the scum of the earth, and I became as they were. I tell you today that who you associate with in life will determine the outcome of your life, good or bad. Please know that!...You be selective about who you choose to associate with. You choose a group that's going somewhere."

Similar situations and others far more sinister happen every weekend in every city in America. Young boys and girls are coerced and even pushed into various sex acts. Elementary and junior high kids are constantly being introduced to alcohol and the most sophisticated, addicting forms of other drugs available. Fighting, stealing, ridiculing others, and cheating run rampant. Simple logic tells us that the fewer times a person is in the presence of such activities, the less his/her chances are of becoming involved. We need to remember that if our social development, particularly in the early and teenage years, is mismanaged, the seeds for negative repercussions that last a lifetime may be sewn. We do become that which we associate with most.

My parents used to tell me, "A friend isn't a friend who will ask you to do something wrong. They are just acquaintances." I really didn't get that phrase for a number of years. I had plenty of *friends* who tried to get me to do bad things for many years. They were a lot of fun to hang around, and they were part of a popular crowd. Now 10 years later, I don't know where most of them are, and they have never made any attempt to keep in touch with me, their old friend. It is only now that I realize how many hundreds of acquaintances I had compared to the small handful of friends who remain.

It is sad to see the great lengths kids will go to to please the acquaintances they innocently mistake for friends. It is also heartbreaking to see the great lengths young boys and girls will go to to please the boyfriend or girlfriend whom they mistakenly view as the *one and only love* of their lives.

Recently many of you may have heard the terrible story of the teenage couple who were allowed to spend nearly every waking moment together. They were grossly over-exposed to each other and were allowed to develop a relationship far too serious for their age. When their parents finally realized that their continual *need* to be together was hindering education and social activities, they demanded that they not see each other any more. Unwilling to be apart, these two kids tragically and dramatically took their lives by jumping into a waterway in a vain attempt to be together forever.

On their own, initially kids do not have the experience required to differentiate between friends and acquaintances or true love and infatuation. Learning to understand the differences between each and learning how to identify and appropriately deal with each is a *Fair Warning* all youth deserve to receive. Having this *Fair Warning* could have helped many of my friends reach their potential rather than spend years stumbling about. Nearly all of my friends who faced serious personal trouble were those who had been allowed to run with whomever they wanted, whenever they wanted, wherever they wanted.

Kids need to have a productive schedule at home. They need exposure to sports, music, church programs, part-time jobs, and other worthwhile extra-curricular activities. Children can then choose among them selecting the one(s) that best meet their talents and interests. Within these kinds of organizations kids meet others who, with their parents support, are choosing to succeed. They too will become achievement oriented. Remember, the least amount of idle time spent with bored kids after school and on the weekends will serve to be the safety net that will literally save their lives. Further, these children will take these experiences with them into adulthood and have developed the wisdom to choose good friends and associates in educational settings as well as financial, political, and business dealings. National statistics indicate that between 3:00PM and 6:00PM is the prime time teenagers commit crimes and get pregnant.

Believe it or not, your little ones one day will look back on their childhood experiences with gratitude for parents who enforced curfews, knew their whereabouts, and knew their friends and acquaintances from their earliest social development.

I knew my old friend, Alex Ruiz, quite well. He was not born a murderer, he became one. He could have become an architect, a school teacher or a policeman. He had great potential. I can't help but wonder what price he would pay today to re-live his youth and pick a new group of friends. How many hundreds of thousands of others throughout the country would also give up everything they now possess to start again and live life knowing how to choose peers and mates?

CHAPTER 6:

Attitudes

Nothing on earth can stop a man with the right attitude from reaching his goals. And nothing on earth can help the man with the wrong attitude.

- Author unknown

The little country schoolhouse was heated by an old-fashioned, pot-bellied coal stove. A little boy had the job of coming to school early each day to start the fire and warm the room before his teacher and his classmates arrived.

One morning they arrived to find the schoolhouse engulfed in flames. They dragged the unconscious little boy out of the flaming building more dead than alive. He had major burns over the lower half of his body and was taken to the nearby county hospital.

From his bed the dreadfully burned, semi-conscious little boy faintly heard the doctor talking to his mother. The doctor told his mother that her son would surely die which was for the best, really, for the terrible fire had devastated the lower half of his body.

But the brave boy did not want to die. He made up his mind that he would survive. Somehow, to the amazement of the physician, he did survive. When the mortal danger was past, he again heard the doctor and his mother speaking quietly. The mother was told that since the fire had destroyed so much flesh in the lower part of his body, it would be almost better if he had died, since he was doomed to be a lifetime cripple with no use at all of his lower limbs.

Once more the brave little boy made up his mind. He would not be a cripple. He would walk. But unfortunately from his waist down, he had no motor ability. His thin legs just dangled there, all but lifeless.

Ultimately he was released from the hospital. Every day his mother would massage his little legs, but there was no feeling, no control, nothing. Yet his determination that he would walk was as strong as ever.

When he wasn't in bed, he was confined to a wheelchair. One sunny day his mother wheeled him out into the yard to get some fresh air. This day, instead of sitting there, he threw himself from his chair. He pulled himself across the grass, dragging his legs behind him.

He worked his way to the white picket fence bordering their lot. With great effort, he raised himself up on the fence. Then, stake by stake, he began dragging himself along the fence, resolved that he would walk. He started to do this every day until he wore a smooth path all around the yard beside the fence. There was nothing he wanted more than to develop life in those legs.

Ultimately through his daily massages, his iron persistence and resolute determination, he did develop the ability to stand up, then to walk haltingly, then to walk by himself— and then — to run.

He began to walk to school, then run to school, to run for the sheer joy of running. Later in college he made the track team.

Still later in Madison Square Garden this young man who was not expected to survive, who would surely never walk, who could never hope to run   —this determined young man, Dr. Glenn Cunningham, ran the world's fastest mile!

> (Chicken Soup for the Soul, as told by Burt Dubin [Deerfield Beach: Health,1993], pp. 259)

If it is possible for such incredible obstacles to be overcome, just think of the many common imperfections of humanity that can be overcome with the right attitude. We all know someone who, if only he/she exhibited a more positive attitude, might do and be much more. These types of individuals would then be living their dreams. They would have more friends and a more meaningful life. M. Russell Ballard said, "Remember, a good attitude produces good results, a fair attitude fair results, a poor attitude poor results. We each shape our own life, and the shape of it is largely determined by our attitude."

The way in which we view certain obstacles or day-to-day tasks greatly determines our moods, effectiveness, stress levels, successes and relationships. Consider the fact that after being cut-off on the freeway, many people arrive at work steaming mad. The tone of their entire day has been set and eventually experienced by everyone around them. When asked how things are going they respond, "Terrible!" or "Oh, it's been one of those days!" In the same situation, many others simply refuse to be affected by such events and will not dwell on circumstances beyond their control. These individuals arrive at work with a pleasant attitude and continue to enjoy the day and remain effective as they handle their responsibilities.

Each year millions rapidly change their lives from mediocre at best to highly successful and deeply meaningful. They do this with a mere change of attitude. They come to the sweeping realization that events and circumstances actually do not control us, but rather our emotional responses to daily events and circumstances determine our specific successes or failings.

I was blessed to learn these truths at a very young age. It didn't immediately sink in, but I eventually learned what it was my parents were trying to teach me. Dad would come home, look at the scowl on my face and ask, "Why are you in such a nasty mood?" I would reply in a huff, "Because Chris and Greg are making me mad!"

"What do you mean, 'making you mad' ?"

I would then complain, "Chris keeps pinching me and Greg took the remote control away."

In retrospect, I find it interesting that before saying a word to the accused, my dad would say to me, "Then why don't you get away from them and go do something else? Don't just sit there and *let yourself* be mad."

Planned or not, Dad taught us very early on that we can change our own circumstances and moods which affect our overall attitude, simply by realizing our situation and doing something about it. In this case, I could get up and leave.

This teaching opportunity was extended before justice was addressed because life is not always just. This teaching opportunity did not provide me with the solution I was seeking, but rather, the solution I needed because life's greatest solutions do not always come the way we want them to. After all, I was the one being pinched and intruded upon. Why should I have to get up and leave? *Because I had the ability to change my circumstances*. Learning to make adjustments when in uncomfortable circumstances is much more valuable than trying in vain to make each and every circumstance comfortable.

This was a preface to the greater, more challenging lesson I would begin to understand later on. That lesson is that many unpleasant circumstances in life are completely out of our control. We cannot just get up and walk out of the room. We must face these challenges head on; we need to deal with them. This requires a higher level of attitude control. It requires the ability to make mental adjustments to be resilient and productive despite difficult circumstances.

In a recent talk, Vaughn J. Featherstone related this important lesson, "Years ago, Russell LeBaron Briggs while Dean of Harvard Law School gave a speech. He told of a student who came in one day, and the Dean asked him why he had not been there the day before to take a test. The student said, 'I wasn't feeling very well, sir.' Dean Briggs said, 'I think you will find, my young friend, that in life most of the work in the world is done by people who are not feeling very well.'" It is this ability to control our attitude even when we aren't feeling like it, that separates the truly great ones from the masses.

What will you do when life's difficulties have been heaped upon you, and you feel hard-pressed to even muster a smile? Will you allow that feeling to take control and lead you into a state of depression? No. Do two things. First, force yourself to smile. If you are all by yourself, force yourself to hum a favorite tune or recall a pleasant memory. You must act as if you are already happy and that will tend to make you happy. Psychologist and philosopher William James put it this way, "Action seems to follow feeling, but really action and feeling go together; and by regulating the action, which is under the more direct control of the will, we can indirectly regulate the feeling, which is not.

"Thus the sovereign voluntary path to cheerfulness, if our cheerfulness be lost, is to sit up cheerfully and to act and speak as if cheerfulness were already there."

Dale Carnegie explained that it is interesting to note that two people may be in the exact same place, that is doing the same job for the same company, earning the same income, living in the same neighborhood in the same city; yet one is miserable, the other happy. Why? Because of their different mental attitudes. We can find just as many happy faces doing backbreaking work in rice fields as we can in the high-income, air-conditioned offices of Los Angeles and New York.

"There is nothing good or bad," said Shakespeare, "but thinking makes it so."

Abe Lincoln once proclaimed, "Most folks are about as happy as they make up their minds to be."

In the classic book *How to Win Friends and Influence*

People, Dale Carnegie shares this story:

> *I saw a vivid illustration as I was walking up the stairs of the*
> *Long Island Railroad station in New York. Directly in front of*
> *me thirty or forty crippled boys on canes and crutches were strug-*
> *gling up the stairs. One boy had to be carried up. I was aston-*
> *ished at their laughter and gaiety. I spoke about it to one of the*
> *men in charge of the boys. "Oh yes," he said, "when a boy real-*
> *izes that he is going to be a cripple for life, he is shocked at first;*
> *but after he gets over the shock, he usually resigns himself to his*
> *fate and then becomes as happy as a normal boy."*

A wonderful father, successful business man, and president
of a large *stake* or area in the Church of Jesus Christ of Latter
Day Saints, Jack Rushton has been loved and admired by thousands over the years. Known not only for his leadership skills
and devotion to his beliefs, but also for his great personality and
excellent sense of humor.

Jack is now known by thousands for his stellar example of
how to move on and continue to achieve greatness through service and inspiration despite unfortunate injuries.

On August 1, 1989, while enjoying an afternoon with his
family in Laguna Beach, California, Jack body-surfed a small,
seemingly harmless wave towards the shore. Unexpectedly, the
wave picked him up and drove him into the sand head first.
Since that day he has been completely paralyzed from the neck
down and respirator dependent.

For several weeks while in the hospital Jack was unable to
communicate his feelings to friends and family. Finally, with
the aid of a special voice monitor, the day arrived that Jack
would utter his first words since the accident. Everyone quietly
gathered around his bed to hear what his response to this ter-

rible life sentence might be. With great effort and without expression, Jack mustered, in strained tones, the following:

"My— name—is—-Jack. I—-broke—my—back!" A beautiful grin stretched across his face. Family and friends laughed and cried with great relief. Jack *was* back!

From that day to this, Jack Rushton truly has been back. He is even more influential and inspirational than before. His cheerful attitude amidst such a trial has helped others reach beyond themselves and become great as well in the process.

A group of church members and neighbors pitched in time, talent, and resources night and day to build a beautiful addition to Jack's home to meet his special needs. Many others sent letters and expressions of love and encouragement. A good friend who served with Jack during his ministry as a stake president continues to visit him nearly every week as he has for the last eight years. There was another family friend who volunteered to come and massage Jack's feet on a regular basis to help stimulate the nerves, to whom Jack once joked, "It is so nice of you to do that for me. It sure looks like it would feel real nice too!"

And then there is his wife, JoAnne, who, without complaint, serves him day and night. Washing, dressing, feeding him, and attending to all of his strenuous and highly specialized needs.

Jack Rushton's resilient attitude combined with service and continued success has proven to edify everyone around him. He inspires others to readjust their attitude about their present situation, whatever it might be.

If situations such as Jack's can breed such positive results, shouldn't we, most of whom will probably never face such a life-altering dilemma, consider how to apply our own attitude to the benefit our day to day challenges.

To illustrate just how a change of attitude in day-to-day responsibilities can change a life forever, I share the story of

Jean Thompson as re-told by Vaughn J. Featherstone:

*On the first day of school, Jean Thompson told her students,
"Boys and girls, I love you all the same." Teachers lie. Little Teddy
Stollard was a boy Jean Thompson did not like. He slouched in his
chair, didn't pay attention, his mouth hung open in a stupor, his
eyes were always unfocused, his clothes were messed, his hair
unkempt, and he smelled. He was an unattractive boy, and Jean
Thompson didn't like him.*

*Teachers have records. And Jean Thompson had Teddy's. First
grade: "Teddy's a good boy. He shows promise in his work and attitude. But he has a poor home situation." Second grade: "Teddy is a
good boy. He does what he is told. But he is too serious. His mother
is terminally ill." Third grade: "Teddy is falling behind in his
work; he needs help. His mother died this year. His father shows no
interest." Fourth grade: "Teddy is in deep waters; he is in need of
psychiatric help. He is totally withdrawn."*

*Christmas came, and the boys and girls brought their presents
and piled them on her desk. They were all in brightly colored paper
except for Teddy's. His was wrapped in brown paper and held
together with scotch tape. And on it, scribbled in crayon, were the
words, "For Miss Thompson from Teddy." She tore open the brown
paper and out fell a rhinestone bracelet with most of the stones missing and a bottle of cheap perfume that was almost empty. When the
other boys and girls began to giggle, she had enough sense to put
some of the perfume on her wrist, put on the bracelet, hold her
wrist up to the children and say, "Doesn't it smell lovely? Isn't the
bracelet pretty?" And taking their cue from the teacher, they all
agreed.*

*At the end of the day, when all of the children had left, Teddy
lingered and came over to the desk and said, "Miss Thompson, all
day long you smelled just like my mother. And her bracelet, that's*

her bracelet, it looks real nice on you too. I'm really glad you liked my presents." And when he left, she got down on her knees and buried her head in her hands and she begged God to forgive her.

The next day when the children came, she was a different teacher. She was a teacher with a heart. And she cared for all the children, but especially those who needed help. Especially Teddy. She tutored him and put herself out for him.

By the end of the year. Teddy had caught up with a lot of the children and was even ahead of some. Several years later, Jean Thompson got this note:

Dear Miss Thompson:
I'm graduating and I'm second in my high school class. I wanted you to be the first to know.
Love, Teddy

Four years later she got another note:
Dear Miss Thompson:
I wanted you to be the first to know. The university has not been easy, but I like it.
Love, Teddy Stollard

Four years later, there was another note:
Dear Miss Thompson:
As of today, I am Theodore J. Stollard, MD. How about that? I wanted you to be the first to know. I'm going to be married in July. I want you to come and sit where my mother would have sat, because you're the only family I have. Dad died last year.
Love, Theodore.

And she went, and she sat where his mother would have sat because she deserved to be there.

The willingness of this good teacher to gather her thoughts, reassess her perspective, and make a conscious decision to change her attitude changed a life forever. Sadly, many people do not realize the potential life-altering effects of the most basic attitude adjustments. Many people equate positive attitude only with dramatic recoveries, financial success or publicized accomplishments.

Attitude is more than that. Attitude is the key to success or failure in all that we do, good or bad, including how we face the most common social dilemmas of the day. It affects the quality of our day-to-day lives. It determines how we live and how we behave. Our attitude shapes our goals and our dreams. It affects all of our relationships, including whether we choose to treat people kindly or not. Attitude can unleash our greatest potential or hide it, as it were, "...under a bushel." *(Matt. 5:15)* Our attitude towards everything we do in life determines our overall happiness.

Consider a broader look at the effects of a good or bad attitude. Children who are not specifically taught to cultivate a positive and resilient attitude will make many unnecessary blunders as they experience life. These blunders have the potential to become extremely serious.

Aside from unfortunate strategic cutbacks, attitude lies at the root of hiring and firing within most companies. The first one hired and the first one fired has almost everything to do with the attitude, which may be discerned through demeanor and self-confidence. The employee's contribution to the company is quickly assessed by the overall quality of his/her work, which is the direct result of that individual's attitude.

Attitude lies at the root of violence as well. Children and adults who engage in any form of violent behavior do so because of an extremely negative attitude about something or someone. (As illustrated in the Pit-Bull incident!) Except for the rare instances of war and self-defense, in my opinion violent behavior is unjustified. Such behavior is brought about by those who choose to cultivate bad attitudes that violently effect those around them. Attitudes of greed, pride and anger finally overflow into various forms of violence.

Attitude lies at the root of underachievement at school. Many kids don't want to, don't have to, or don't think they can; so poor performance and bad grades naturally follow. Such an unproductive attitude may now easily follow them into the workplace if they ever make it there.

Attitude lies at the root of a number of emotional problems including eating disorders, compulsive behaviors, and depression. The young girl or boy who is unreasonably concerned with appearance and personal attention may develop these traits and will act out in a variety of difficult-to-correct, destructive ways. All of this begins when positive attitudes are not developed or when winsome attitudes are replaced with self-doubt and negativity. A recent survey indicates that nearly 45% of nine year-olds had dieted because of parental comments and suggestions concerning their appearance. Emotional problems such as these can turn bright, young kids into truly desperate and self-destructive persons.

Attitude lies at the root of racism. Many people cannot see past skin color or a regional accent. Those who cannot look past certain aspects of birth and background lend themselves to yet another social dilemma and may miss out on opportunities for true success and happiness in life. They have a real attitude problem.

Many parents focus so much on the day-to-day tasks of life and the physical aspects of parenting such as chores, homework, dropping off and picking up from various activities; getting dinner ready; and tending to their own needs that they pass up many valuable teaching opportunities concerning attitude. Most people simply forget how important attitude really is or never even think to address it. These teaching opportunities may be indirect daily experiences such as the one described in the story of my brother and my father earlier in the chapter. These teaching opportunities can be extended by simply sharing experiences and stories, encouraging, complimenting, and genuinely praising your children and by addressing a child's negative attitude when displayed.

Before teaching a young one to have a good attitude about various principles of life, you must identify your own personal perspectives. Find out what your perspectives are and your attitude about specific situations reveals itself. What were you taught about honesty while growing up? Was it strictly enforced or rarely discussed? What kind of attitude did you see in your parents? Were they complainers, excuse makers, and arguers or were they productive achievers and peacemakers? What were you taught about race? Did you hear a lot of condescension pertaining to other ethnicities? Did your parents encourage you to have friends based on values and common interests rather than race and/or religion? Were you ever in the home of a person of another race? Again, find your perspective, and likely, your attitude will simultaneously bear out.

When attempting to instill a positive attitude within children, it is vital that they have a healthy perspective. Without it, their attitudes will be greatly inhibited. To illustrate this, refer to the previous paragraph: When dishonesty is taken lightly, a child takes it lightly when personally confronted with it. That is a bad attitude to have. When complaining, excuse making, and arguing are the norm amongst parents, children perceive they are acceptable. They will develop a complaining, blaming, and argumentative attitude.

If prejudice is allowed and exhibited through mean, untrue, and derogatory speech; a child perceives that he or she is actually better than another group of people. They develop an attitude of racism. This process is repeated again and again for all of the innumerable attitudes one acquires. Present healthy perspectives, change unhealthy ones, and a more healthy, resilient and positive attitude will follow.

A story is told by David B. Haight of a young man who was serving in the second world war. During a time of training and preparation he sent a letter to his family, a portion of which reads:

> *...for the last three days we have practiced throwing hand grenades.*
> *I have been able to throw the grenade as far as thirty feet.*
> *Today they gave us live grenades. I got eighty-five feet!*

This is an excellent example of how personal perception greatly affects attitude, and ultimately our day-to-day performance. The reality of imminent danger certainly changed this young man's perspective, his attitude, and his performance!

As parents, it is our responsibility to teach the truths and realities of life. We do this so that our children will gain an appropriate perspective of right and wrong. Each of us, in our heart of hearts, understands these truths. We have been there. We have experienced the pleasure and pain of our decisions, which in turn, have made us aware of what is right and what is wrong. In most cases, we know the difference between right and wrong, and whatever our decision is, whether we choose to do the right thing or the wrong thing, does not alter that fact in any way. We all know that we should not gossip, backbite, complain, cheat, steal, curse, demean, or manipulate. We all know that we should learn to exhibit self-control and foster kindness, honesty, graciousness, devotion, virtue, and selflessness. We have the ability within us to extend the most beneficial and healthy perspectives on life and the ability to extend *Fair Warnings* for the development of a truly positive attitude. Healthy perspectives affect our children's overall attitudes, which come to the forefront as they face the multitude of life's challenges.

Millions of people live lives contrary to what they know in their heart is right and best for the soul. Turmoil, the direct result of their own poor decisions, surrounds them. The turmoil continues despite the fact that before making the poor decisions, they really *knew better* but did it anyway. It is nearly impossible for these people to significantly teach the principles, the *Fair Warnings*, if they have not yet mastered or begun to master the principles they are attempting to teach their children. Instead they present a confusing, contradictory perspective to the child. When teaching a young boy to control his temper after an angry outburst, mom or dad must possess the self-discipline required to control their own angry outbursts. Thus, parents must present a consistent perspective of the principle while their offspring develop a healthy attitude about it.

For those who seem or feel trapped by their personal shortcomings, I recall the *paradigm shift* as explained in Dr. Stephen R. Covey's book, *Principle-Centered Leadership*. He describes a paradigm as, "...your scheme for understanding and explaining certain aspects of reality." A paradigm shift then, is a change in the explanation and understanding or a breakthrough in one's approach toward friends, family, decision-making, etc. In other words, "...breaks with old ways of thinking."

An old-time banker might have had a sharp paradigm shift had he the opportunity to catch a glimpse of our day. To an eager investor he confidently counseled, "My friend, hold on to that money. The car is just another fad; the horse is here to stay!"

Some of your personal flaws may not seem too significant at this point. Or you might not see any real reason to change. A deeper, more honest look may reveal a new angle, an entirely new way of thinking. You might ask yourself: What are my weaknesses? How will my weaknesses affect my children? My spouse? How much better could I be if I took control of my weaknesses? What might be the result if I get professional help for a detrimental, life-long habit? These probing questions, along with input from loved ones may spark the needed shift of perspective or *paradigm shift* spurring you into action, bringing about immediate changes, preparing you for greater influence and respect within your home. If you have difficulty committing to become a better individual, this introspection is a step to take now to help you qualify to teach all of the truths you want and know your children eventually need to acquire.

This report was circulated on the internet this year, "In Bowling Green, Ohio, student Robert Ricketts, 19, had his head bloodied when he was struck by a Conrail train. He told police he was trying to see how close to the moving train he could place his head without getting hit."

I use this ridiculous story to point out that we act just as foolishly as Robert when we continue to act in ways which have proven ineffective time and time again. When we recognize and accept that we continue doing the things which we *know* we are much *better* without, we are ready for change. It might be time for a great personal *paradigm shift.*

However, this undertaking is by no means easy. The willingness to make sacrifices and shed weaknesses in the form of bad habits and unhealthy perspectives is a lifelong effort. The results derived from such pursuits benefit so many beyond oneself, parents, siblings, spouse, children and co-workers. When we commit to making our lives better is when we are most effective teaching our children what it means as well as the challenges involved in bringing about a good attitude. With the added value of example, you more effectively teach them that paying the price for a disciplined mind, disciplined behavior, and a positive attitude can allow them to literally create greatness from any set of circumstances they are given in life. That understanding will carry them through all of their obstacles and trials to the realization of their greatest ambitions.

Shana and I are trying to raise our girls with a correct perspective of right and wrong so that they too will have the best outlook and attitude when faced with their critical decisions in life. If we succeed, they will have an air of healthy optimism, which will help them refuse to be involved in the activities and behaviors they have learned are detrimental to them. And when difficulties and obstacles come their way, they will have the valuable ability to see the good in every hand they are dealt throughout life.

That quality of optimism, or positive attitude is illustrated nicely in this little story found in *More Sower's Seeds* about twin boys. One a complaining pessimist. The other, a forever optimist:

> *Concerned about their differences, the parents decide to take their boys to a local psychologist.*
>
> *After several evaluations, the psychologist suggests a plan to balance the twin's personalities. "On their next birthday," he advises, "put them in separate rooms to open their gifts. Give the pessimist the best toys you can afford, and give the optimist a box of manure." The parents follow the instructions and carefully observe the results.*
>
> *The parents watch as the pessimist eagerly opens his present. Inside he found a new computer and a great new video game. Immediately the little boy says aloud, "This is the OLD comput-*

*er! And I don't even like this game; I know someone who has a
much nicer computer than this."*

*Disappointed, the parents meander down the hall to
watch the second little boy open his present. They peek inside
his room and find the little boy gleefully digging through the
box of manure and throwing it up in the air. Giggling, he
says, "You can't fool me! Where there's this much manure,
there's gotta be a pony!"*

Maybe this boy was a little disillusioned in his optimism, but
I think he'll go places in years to come. With an attitude like that,
there will be little chance of changing his perspective and steer-
ing him away from his goals and decisions to do the right thing.

This *Fair Warning* of positive attitude is absolutely vital. It
will affect every aspect of a person's life. Not only will your children begin to cultivate a mind set, which will help them through
life's tragedies; but more practically, they will know how to effectively maneuver through life's daily challenges. It may eventually be the ignition needed to be successful in making your *"...Own
Good Children Great."*

CHAPTER 7:

Hard Work, Honesty, and the Truth About Money

Work is honorable. It is good therapy for most problems. It is the antidote for worry. Work makes it possible for the average to approach genius. When work and duty and joy are commingled, then man is at his best.

- J. Richard Clarke

This is rather hard to admit, but as a kid I was unusually resistant to work or, perhaps I should say, to hard labor. I know, most kids don't beg to go out and bundle branches, pull weeds and get the yard cleaned up. But most kids don't cry about it either when they are 14 years old. I did. And I don't mean *whine.* I mean really crying, unable to catch my breath crying. Blubbering, actually. I ended up having to do the work, but with tear-stained eyes and slobbery sleeves. None of my friends ever knew of my extended years of childlike wailing. It was one of our family secrets. A Chavez family skeleton.

Part of this emotional problem was due to the trauma sustained while temporarily employed by family friends. You see, not only did I resist working initially, but once I began, it became evident that I wasn't all that efficient.

On one occasion, while working for our good friend, Dave, I was given a simple, singular assignment. Dave was clearing avocado trees from his lot with a backhoe. Another worker was cutting all of the branches into small pieces. My assignment was to bundle, drag, and throw the debris into the large trash bin.

Everything was going just fine for a couple hours. At that point my mind began to wander a little. I was now throwing the sticks into the bin, one at a time, imagining that I was pitching strikes and throwing martial arts weaponry. I abandoned the bundling technique. This was because I thought I was doing the job too quickly, I was afraid Dave would tell me to do something else, like dig a trench. So I lollygagged a bit. (This is part of the efficiency deficit alluded to earlier.)

After finding one particularly gnarly, knotted branch, I quickly whipped around and winged it toward the bin. This particular branch was in a C-shape, and it sort of hooked off my hand and veered off to the right, just missing the bin and squarely hitting our friend, Ken, in the forehead. He collapsed like a wet noodle as blood oozed out of the gash.

Ken survived after receiving a few stitches. Dave lost about $600 that day thanks to me. It was the last time I was employed on that job-site.

On another occasion I was asked to baby-sit two young boys, about 7 and 9 years old. The parents told me they would play nicely outside and I would just have to watch out for them.

The parents had been gone for only 20 minutes when I decided to go inside to make a quick phone call. I needed to arrange a ride to the beach for the following morning. Obviously, a very urgent and justified phone call. Within minutes I heard a terrible shriek of pain in the front yard. In ran the younger boy, followed by his guilty looking big brother. The little boy was holding his arm crying and screaming, "I hurt my arm! I hurt my arm!" I asked if I could see, and he held out his little limb. As soon as he held it out, it swooped down and bent as if he had an additional joint between his wrist and elbow. My blood ran cold, I thought I would vomit.

After scrambling to find a way over to the hospital, I sat in the emergency room for about five hours waiting for his mother and father to arrive. My anxiety about explaining the event to them was compounded by the sad yelping and crying that continued as the medical staff worked to set his little bones. When his mom and dad finally arrived, they were exceedingly merciful and understanding. So much so that they asked if I could watch the boys the next weekend. I declined. I officially retired from all employment on that day.

However, while in retirement, thankfully, my mom provided a situation which forced me to continue to learn the value of work and responsibility.

Soon after I turned 12, one day my mom called me to come down to the the laundry room. She handed me a box of detergent, threw a load of my dirty clothes onto the washer and abruptly announced, "You are now going to do your own laundry!" Curiously I asked, "Oh, you mean,...today?" "No," she said, "Forevermore!" Without giving me an opportunity to begin my certain tirade of complaints, she said, "Divide your clothes into piles of whites, darks, and everything in between, and throw them in the washer separately, along with one scoop of detergent. Then, you just turn the knob to this line, close the door, and push start. As soon as it's done, put everything in the dryer, close the door, turn the knob to 'High' and hit 'Start.' I squeaked in, "But, I..." Quickly she interrupted, "And be sure to get them out of the dryer soon or they'll be wrinkled. Don't mix any colors with your whites. Plan on losing socks." She left the room, and I was a changed boy.

I quickly realized that this was one chore I could not avoid. Wearing dirty clothes was simply not acceptable! Apparently, even young kids do not appreciate the stench of dirty, wrinkled clothes. I tried to disguise the odor with Jean Nate roll-on deodorant, but it just didn't work. I was losing friends and losing them fast. I was forced to adjust my attitude and get the job done.

Eventually I restored old friendships, but ended up with a closet full of wrinkled, pink church shirts and a drawer full of pink underwear. Throughout that school year I rarely wore a set of matching socks, but I was slowly learning to work.

At 15 or 16 I finally snapped out of it. I got a job as a dishwasher and then a busboy. I ran the early shift at the local donut store, served frozen yogurt with a smile at *Checkers*, and drove a delivery route for a wholesale flower company.

Work was required, and I was beginning to understand the value of it. Now responsible for certain tasks, I began to recognize the benefit of honesty. I began to recognize that our honesty is tested nearly every day we are asked to give an honest day's work for an honest day's wage.

The issue of honesty seems to surface very early. Who teaches kids to fib? I don't know who does initially, but children sure become aware of this tactic early on.

When my wife was around 5 or 6 years old, she was sternly confronted by her very annoyed mother who was holding *The Holy Bible* in her hand. Waving the *Bible* she asked, "Shana, did you use a marker on this book?" Innocently, with her freckled little face Shana looked up and said, "No. Why?" "Because somebody has written across the inside of this book. And do you want to see what it says?"

Her mom turned the page and let her take a look. Scrawled across the introduction to Genisis in deep purple marker was the word, Shana. The evidence was quite convincing. Shana had been caught in a fib.

I was similarly indicted between my 5th and 6th years.

While supposedly taking a nap, I crept into the hallway while my mother was in the other room packing boxes for our move. I came across my mom's purse sitting on a chair. For whatever reason, I opened her wallet, took out all of the bills and stashed them away.

With the goods hidden, I denied any involvement when asked if I knew anything about the missing money. The mystery continued for two or three days, and I began to grasp the seriousness when I overheard my parents discussing, "hundreds of dollars."

Finally, in an attempt to pull it off, I decided to show my big brother some money that I, "...found over at the park. I was digging under the play spaceship and found it in the sand." I casually told him, "You can have it if you want."

I did the best I could to get rid of the goods, but like my sneaky little wife-to-be, I had a pretty strong case stacked against me. I never would have guessed that my brother Chris was actually an informant.

It seems to me that the nature of youth begs to be taught. Young kids do dumb things and are continually placing themselves in positions to learn. Unfortunately, too many parents don't take advantage of these glaring opportunities. They don't sit down and actually talk to their children about the value and necessity of honesty.

As previously illustrated, the indiscretions of youth can be laughable. Left uncorrected though, they can become extremely serious as our responsibilities increase. This truth manifested itself recently in my business.

I was glad to hire Todd. He was young, ambitious, and a self-proclaimed religious man. He was a great salesperson and seemed to have a consistent work ethic. As he continued working with me, we became friends and I trusted him.

About 18 months after he began, there was an incident that caused me to question his integrity. I looked into the matter and became aware of a most unethical scheme he had masterminded whereby he was providing proprietary information to a local competitor for a fee. Todd was stealing from us. Once we were absolutely certain what was happening, I personally confronted him with our information. Todd flatly denied any involvement. Despite our multiple eyewitness sources and various documents, he claimed to be innocent and continued to do so even after he was fired.

Todd's act of dishonesty left him unemployed with no time to prepare or plan for his future. He's lucky he didn't end up in jail. He might not have lost his job had he confessed and faced up to the charges. He added insult to injury by compounding his dishonesty through denial.

This sort of dishonesty, which years earlier, may have been passed off as a laughable indiscretion, had grown into a serious problem for this young father. Who knows when the problem began for him, he probably succeeded in similar cases of dishonesty and irresponsibility for many years. But, as is almost always the case, his acts of dishonesty finally found their way to the surface. Eventually the dishonest person forgets to cover up something along the way, forgets who has been told what and finally gets caught.

In another example, Scott, a very close family friend, decided to accept the *Monster Burrito Challenge* at a local Mexican restaurant. The challenge was for one person to eat an 8 lb. concoction of beans, sour cream, guacamole, chiles, beef, and jalepenos within one hour. The reward for meeting the challenge was a crisp $100 bill.

As the hour came to a close, you could see the whites of his eyes had actually turned bean brown. He was ill and fighting regurgitation with every mouthful. And furthermore, he was not even close to finishing the *Monster*.

Unwilling to concede defeat, Scott concocted a plan. In his mind, Scott convinced himself that the *Monster Burrito* was, in fact, a concoction of leftovers assembled at the direction of management. The *Monster Burrito* was made up of dried out, left-over re-fried beans; dangerously hot chiles; and way too much sour cream of indeterminate origin. Thus, Scott believed that he had been *tricked* into eating a burrito with no appealing palatable qualities whatsoever. As he sat in the hot sun with only a small glass of water to quench his thirst, he became convinced his failure was the restaurant's plan.

Feeling justified and still determined to win, Scott began to break off large chunks of the *Monster Burrito* and throw them up on the patio cover next to him. After discarding enough of the burrito to be able to finish the remainder on his own, a small crowd of customers and employees gathered round to witness the so-called accomplishment. Suddenly, there was an awful ruckus on top of the patio cover.

Some seagulls had spotted the remains of the burrito laid out just above Scott's table. Now in a feeding frenzy, 10 or more seagulls swarmed and swooped about scavenging what Scott had tossed up there.With great ferocity, the seagulls fought over these remains causing a terrible commotion. Bits of tortilla and beans scattered about, some even falling back onto Scott's table. It was obvious to all that the burrito fragments bore an uncanny resemblance to the *Monster Burrito*.

Scott lost out on being the first to conquer the *Monster*. He left with nothing more than a greatly upset stomach and the request, "...please don't come back." Actually Scott is a very noble person. That day though, probably brought on by bean overload, he suffered a brief lapse of judgement. Nevertheless, he was reminded that deceit makes itself known in the end.

A young person needs to understand that dishonesty will never bring the results he/she seeks. Moreover, we all must learn that we need to work very hard for what we want in life. Combining a strict and unwavering attitude towards honesty with hard work, we will be valued and successful in all that we do. Adding a healthy understanding about money to honesty and a solid work ethic usually leads to the creation of very wise and wealthy individuals.

The healthy understanding about money I refer to is not complex. It is the basic understanding that nothing is free. It is the realization that you must work hard for everything you desire financially. It is a realization that material wealth alone does not constitute success, and the recognition received by he who attains wealth by compromising honesty and integrity is not wealthy after all. It is a basic understanding that greed, envy and jealousy towards the possessions of others is unhealthy and detrimental to your ability to build your own financial foundation.

If our old employee, Todd, had had a healthy understanding about money, he might not have felt the desire to get ahead through a deceitful short-cut, which really was no short-cut at all. If more children of my generation and the generation before us had been extended such an understanding, we might have many more self sustaining Americans and far fewer crowding our jails. So many are convicted for a multitude of crimes which directly stem from dishonesty and financial short-cuts.

It is necessary to understand these concepts as early as possible so they may take root and become, with time, the values that make up what that person stands for. Without these deep convictions, one may find him/herself in a critical moment of compromise that can become a terrible turning point in an otherwise successful and accomplished life. Sometimes this occurs in a moment of stress or desperation when the serious trials of life are upon us. And eventually, the serious trials of life visit all of us. Phillips Brooks once said, "Some day in the years to come, you will be wrestling with the great temptation, or trembling under the great sorrow of your life. But the real struggle is here, now. Now it is being decided whether, in the day of your supreme sorrow or great temptation, you shall miserably fail or gloriously conquer. Character cannot be made except by a steady, long, continued process."

Those of us in Southern California can easily recall the Orange County (California) bankruptcy of 1995. Over a billion dollars was lost, $1.64 billion to be exact, through a risky, dishonest, misleading investment situation overseen by the former Treasurer, Robert Citron. Prior to these events, the Treasurer had what appeared to be an accomplished life and career. But it would seem, the most basic forms of pride, greed, and dishonesty grew into an overwhelming financial debacle, which could not be overcome. On April 27, 1995, he pled guilty to six felonies and in November of 1996 was sentenced to one year in prison along with a $100,000 fine.

At that critical moment of decision, when the Treasurer allowed any degree of deception, he failed his personal test of character, and the results were far reaching. So far reaching, in fact, that Citron later wrote, "After I resigned...and after the bankruptcy, I contemplated suicide."

Upon sentencing, Superior Court Judge J. Stephen Czuleger said concerning this former official, "He put himself in this position. He chose to engage in the type of activity over the years that he did. It caught up with him. It overcame him. And it ultimately came close to destroying him." (*The Orange County Register*, Nov. 20, 1996)

I firmly believe that parents can help their children be firm in their commitment to the previously mentioned principles before they are confronted with compromising situations of such magnitude. Some parents do well in teaching their kids to work hard and be honest. However, they altogether neglect to teach them anything about the nature of money; how it can be used for wealth or ruin.

Consider the ease of credit card use. As soon as a person earns the most meager wages, they are faced with the ever persuasive enticement to "...buy now, pay later," all with the swipe of a card. As we all know, millions go overboard with this concept and quickly find themselves in a deep financial bind.

Why not take some time to explain the basics of the financial system before sending the children off to college? Why not set up a savings program for them, which the kids contribute to? Why not loan them a little money with interest, and teach them what happens when they overextend themselves?

Financial conflict is one of the most significant factors contributing to divorce. Erratic spending habits, mis-management, poor work ethic, greed, and dishonesty are often the cause of some terribly damaging arguments that strike at the foundation of a marriage and a family.

Kids deserve a *Fair Warning* concerning such things. And the sooner, the better. In October, 1994, *Reader's Digest* featured an article entitled *Cheating In Our Schools: A National Scandal*. This article revealed an alarming attitude of American youth concerning honesty. "Honesty and integrity have been replaced in many classrooms by a win-at-any-cost attitude that puts grades, expediency and personal gain above all else. 'Moral standards have become so eroded that many children can no longer tell right from wrong,' says Kevin Ryan, founding director of the Center for the Advancement of Ethics and Character at Boston University."

In the article educational psychologist, Fred Schab, shared his 1969 and 1989 surveys of high school students. In 1969, 34% admitted cheating on tests; by 1989 that figure had doubled. In 1969, 58% of students let other students copy their homework; by 1989, 98% said they had.

One student commented, "Cheating has become a guiltless type of thing. Ten minutes cheating is better than two hours studying." When one teacher was asked why he tolerated such widespread cheating he gave this shocking reply, "If we stopped our students from cheating, they would be at a competitive disadvantage."

The article concludes with these words of wisdom from Al Burr, a former public high school principal, "We need to focus on producing young adults who know how to behave when nobody's watching." And from Jay Mulkey, president of the non-profit Character Education Institute in San Antonio, TX, who states, "Cheating is habit forming. Students who cheat in class may well cheat in their jobs or on their spouses. When you have a country that doesn't value honesty and thinks character is unimportant, what kind of society do you have?"

Show your children how to work. Teach them the value of strict honesty. Share with them your experiences about the dangerous disillusionments associated with money.

If you never see your teenager studying, and he/she brings home a 3.5 GPA (grade point average), please don't flatter yourself. He or she may have learned the convenience of cheating. It is up to you, the parent, to teach your children why they shouldn't.

I had a friend who brought home a 3.5 GPA that way. He was accepted by one of the prestigious University of California campuses. His parents were overjoyed and very proud. When he arrived on campus, he had no idea what he was doing. After one year, he had completely flunked out. For the time being, he is another statistic among the complacent segment of *Generation X*.

Teach the next generation the deep values of hard work, honesty, and the truth about money. Let them know they may not get everything they want when they want it. And although they may have to forego some of the immediate pleasures, with time they will have the lasting benefits of true joy and personal satisfaction that accompanies real achievement. With time, their odds for occupational security and a valuable net worth will be immeasurably enhanced. They will come to appreciate the words of Florence Nightengale who wrote:

I slept and dreamt that life was joy;
I awoke and found that life was duty;
I acted;
Behold, in duty was joy!

CHAPTER 8:

Media

Nearly all parents want to convey to their children the importance of self-discipline, hard work, and decent manners; but the entertainment media celebrate vulgar behavior, contempt for all authority, and obscene language— which is inserted even in 'family fare' where it is least expected.

- Micheal Medved, author of Hollywood vs. America

FATHER'S DAY IN TELEVISION LAND, 1957:
Bud has a problem. His coach just cut him from the team. He goes to his wise, calm and wonderful father who offers him some sage advice, such as "Try, try again." Bud realizes that father indeed knows best, He follows pop's advice and becomes the star of the team.

FATHER'S DAY IN TELEVISION LAND, 1997:
Bart has a problem. In fact, Bart is a problem. He seeks advice from anyone and everyone but Homer, since dad doesn't know a darn thing. This is confirmed when Homer finally offers Bart direction, based on his own life views. "If something is too hard, give it up. The moral, my boy is to never try anything."

(Paula Hunker, June 1997, The Washington Times.)

In many ways the media, i.e.TV, radio, movies, magazines, and the internet, have become the *guardians* or *sitters* of American youth. The ease by which the media is accessed and enjoyed make for a dangerously simple way to occupy time and for parents to find a little relief from demanding children. Media can be educational, instructional, and can provide healthy entertainment. But, as in all things, overexposure without oversight can lead to problems.

Consider the serious repercussions of the following example of parental carelessness and irresponsibility concerning explicit materials available to unsupervised youth.

I was in fifth or sixth grade when one day I walked into Jason's house after school and heard his older brothers laughing and snickering in the living room. "Hey you guys, come in here and look at this!" We walked over and my eyes must have been as wide as silver dollars when I viewed the scene which had the undivided attention of the four or five older boys in the room.

Their dad always left a stack of hard-core pornographic videos behind the TV. And these boys were familiar with them all. In addition, there was a two-foot stack of pornographic magazines sitting on a bookshelf in plain view. In retrospect, recalling the lack of structure and supervision, I am not at all surprised that by the eighth grade, Jason was having sex at his house before his parents came home from work. During high school his girlfriend had her first abortion.

A recent report indicated that 76% of adults think that individual behavior is the overriding factor contributing to many of the current problems we face as a society. Ironically, of those respondents only 11% felt that their personal behavior has had any negative effect on society. Of course, it is always somebody else. I would wager that Jason's parents don't feel they are part of the problem either. In my opinion, any parent who makes little or no effort to regulate the use and consumption of media within the home is a significant part of the problem.

A 1991 survey taken by Mellman and Lazarus, *American*

Family Values Study: A Return to Family Values, reveals that only 2% of respondents think that television *should* have the greatest influence on their children's values, but 56% believe, in fact, that it does have the greatest influence, more than parents, teachers, and religious leaders combined. Can this really be true? Can the media actually be affecting and influencing America's youth to such a degree?

In search of answers to these questions I found some rather stunning statistics, some of which may be common knowledge and some which may not. The following information comes from an excellent talk entitled, Ancient and Modern Idolatry, given by Randal A. Wright, Ph.D., at the educational CES Symposium held at Brigham Young University in 1995. Randal A. Wright has spent over 20 years researching the effect of the media on family, has written several books on the subject and is considered an expert in this particular area of study.

In Mr. Wright's talk he shares statistics from a 1994 article featured in *USA Today*. The report indicated that 1,490 hours were spent each year watching TV, or 4 hours each day; 1,380 hours were spent listening to radio, music, and CDs, or 3.7 hours each day; 46 hours, or about 1 hour each week, was spent at the movie theater or watching videos. Thus, the average American places himself or herself under the direct influence of the media for 2,916 hours a year or 56 hours each week!

Does the media influence us? Can the media really have more influence than parents, teachers, and religious leaders combined? Yes, when we allow it to.

Mr. Wright quoted Spencer W. Kimball who wisely said, "Man is naturally a religious being. His heart instinctively seeks for God. Whether he reverences the sacred cow or prays to the sun or the moon; whether he kneels before wood or stone images or prays in secret to his Father in Heaven, he is satisfying an inborn urge to look to someone bigger than us." He then proceeded to point out that the media marketers play on that truth. They have mastered the art of capturing our attention and sounding their message in our ears. They have set up *heroes* for our viewing pleasure, and we gladly *worship*.

In one of his books, *Why Do Good People See Bad Movies?*, Randal A. Wright shares the findings of Dorthy Barclay who documented startling differences in the heroes of society between 1900 and 1950. In 1900, the participants in this study listed their heroes as follows:

78% Historical figures
12% Literary figures
10% Relatives and acquaintances

In 1950 a new element had arrived on the scene and in less than a lifetime a dramatic change had taken place. The results follow:

33% Historical figures
0% Literary figures
10% Relatives
57% Movie, TV, Music and Sports stars
(*Dorthy Barclay, Youth's Heroes and Hero Worship*, [The New York Times Magazine], Nov 1951, pp.42)

In his book, Mr. Wright provided some extremely insightful statistics which came from his own extensive survey of American youth concerning media consumption and its effects. On of several questions asked was, "If you could trade places with anyone, who would it be?" The results? Seventeen of the top 20 named were TV and movie personalities. The second largest group mentioned came from the music industry. The third largest group named were figures in the world of professional sports. (*Why Do Good People See Bad Movies?*, [National Family Institute, 1993] pp.13-15)

Aside from this study and others like it, how do we really know how much these people are admired? How can we measure their influence? One way is by looking at the money we pay them to entertain us.

Citing an article published in *USA Today*, May 1993, Mr. Wright illustrated that in 1982 the starting salary for the average American worker was $21,077. In 1991 that salary had risen to $29,421. By comparison, in 1982 the average professional basketball player earned a salary of $235,000, and by 1991 that salary had increased to $1,041,667. (*ibid.*)

Here are the highest paid athletes of 1996 as estimated by *Forbes* in their Dec. 16, 1996 issue (in millions):

PERSON	SPORT	SALARY	ENDORSE	TOTAL
1. Mike Tyson	Boxing	75.0	0.0	75.0
2. Michael Jordan	Basketball	12.6	40.0	52.6
3. Michael Schumacher	Auto racing	25.0	8.0	33.0
4. Shaquille O'Neal	Basketball	7.4	17.0	24.4
5. Emmitt Smith	Football	13.0	3.5	16.5
6. Evander Holyfield	Boxing	15.0	0.5	15.5
7. Andre Agassi	Tennis	2.2	13.0	15.2
8. Arnold Palmer	Golf	0.1	15.0	15.1
9. Dennis Rodman	Basketball	3.9	9.0	12.9
10. Patrick Ewing	Basketball	10.9	1.5	12.4

When Tiger Woods made his official entrance into the world of professional golf with his historic greeting, "Hello world," he was enthusiastically welcomed with endorsements estimated in excess of $60 million. Why such revenues? Because we are willing to pay that price. The revenues are proof of the influence.

In the talk I mentioned earlier, Mr. Wright made a great point with this thought, "E.T. ate a piece of candy. What was it called? ...*Reese's Pieces* And their *(Reese's Pieces')* sales went up 78% the next month... In 1985, for some strange reason the number of young men who applied to be navy fighter pilots increased dramatically. Did the movie *Top Gun* have anything to do with it? In 1993, for some strange reason, the number of people who visited and donated to dinosaur museums just skyrocketed. Why? *Jurassic Park*? Maybe. *Barney*? Maybe...Are we influenced? I believe we are."

Now, what happens when one of these heroes decides to glamorize alcohol, drugs, and promiscuity? What happens when one of them exhibits public anger, disrespect, and rudeness? What message is sent when Roberto Alomar spits in an umpires face in front of millions of onlookers? What message is sent when Dennis Rodman head-butts a referee and kicks a photographer? What message is sent when Christian Slater, Charlie Sheen, Robert Downey Jr. and a host of others in the spotlight are hauled off to jail? What are children learning from the likes of Marilyn Manson who openly preaches Satanism through his music and interviews?

And what of TV and movie content? Can children really be influenced that heavily by it? Well here again, we only need to look at the revenues which proves the influence to answer that question. Today the stars of sitcoms can earn between $50 thousand and $1 million *per episode*. Several movie stars can demand between $5 million and $30 million *per movie*. We pay the fees as we watch with every increasing frequency. Proof that we are heavily influenced.

In his book, *The Index of Leading Cultural Indicators*, William

Bennett reminds us of another study performed by *USA Today*. In this study, *USA Today* staff members watched one week of prime-time television on ABC, NBC, CBS, and FOX. Among the findings:

- Of the 45 sex scenes shown on network television, 23 were between unmarried heterosexual couples, 16 were adulterous, 4 were between married heterosexuals, 1 involved a homosexual couple, and 1 involved unmarried, heterosexual teens.

- Among the 94 shows watched, 48 showed at least one violent act. All told there were 276 acts of violence in which 57 people were killed and 99 people were assaulted.

- Although 60 percent of Americans "never doubt the existence of God" and 42 percent attend church once a week, only 5 percent of TV characters practice any religion in any form.

If our children find their heroes in the media, then, overwhelmingly, these are the messages that you should expect them to receive. Yes, there are some people in professional sports and in the music and movie industries who set stellar examples. There are a handful who use their positions of influence for good. We know who they are because they stand apart from the rest, but they usually don't get quite as much attention as the ones who peddle trash. And we all know which athletes and stars peddle trash, yet unfortunately, they are some of the most popular people in their fields.

Hero-worship is defined in the dictionary as the "idealization of an admired man or woman." (*Readers Digest Oxford,* 1996) The definition of a hero is "a person noted or admired for nobility, courage, and outstanding achievements." (*ibid.*) I am afraid people today have forgotten that a hero is a person who represents goodness, nobility, courage, and outstanding achievement. I am afraid that in this clever world of mass-marketing, hundreds of less-than-heroic people are being accepted as the heroes of the American public.

We know that to worship someone or some message takes sacrifice. We give up time, money and effort to be considered a true follower or one who worships. If this is true, then the facts and figures of time and money spent on every media source by America, makes us a nation of media worshippers. It is a frightening thought.

Plato once said that, "Musical training is a more potent instrument than any other, because rhythm and harmony find their way into the inward places of the soul, on which they mightily fasten, imparting grace." Also in Mr. Bennett's book, are some intriguing statistics in reference to music consumption and content:

> - *Fifteen to nineteen-year-olds buy more music than any other monitored age group.*
> - *Between the seventh and twelfth grades, the average teenager listens to 10,500 hours of rock music, just slightly less than the entire number of hours spent in the classroom from kindergarten through high school.*
>
> - *In one popular album which sold 1.7 million copies, there were 226 uses of the word f-word, 81 uses of the s-word, 163 uses of the word bitch, 87 descriptions of oral sex, and 117 explicit terms for male or female genitalia.*
> *(The Index of Leading Cultural Indicators, [Touchstone; New York, 1994]pp.104-112)*

We know that the powers of media specifically target the young people who will make up the next generation of media consumers. Recently in *George Magazine*, Jonathan Bernstein asked, "Does anyone these days launch a big-budget movie, album, television show or software without factoring teen appeal into the equation? Doubtful. The kids have the disposable income, they've got the free time, and they've got the obsessive nature."

Jon Nesvig, president of the advertising for FOX, was blunt when he said, "We're selling the next generation of customers." And at FOX, they keep the attention of the next generation by airing the likes of *Married With Children*, which is the longest running sitcom on television.

In one episode of this show, as documented in the May 1996 issue of *Reader's Digest*, the father and son rhapsodize about an upcoming trip to "the nudie bar, where you see their butt and their trap stays shut." And apparently, parents aren't turning the TV off despite the fact that this sort of dialogue is repeated over and over again each night and on every major network. As one critic noted in the same issue, "do it" is a more common television expression than "stay tuned."

The facts cannot be disputed, the media has an overwhelming impact on children, teens, and the entire society. Merely viewing and listening to the depictions and innuendos of various sex acts, drug use, and violence may seem harmless to some parents. "Oh, my kids won't go off and do all that" may be the rationalization. But they will never really know until it happens. They can never know their children's weaknesses and proclivities until they rear their ugly heads. In regard to *merely* viewing and listening, these parents either forget or altogether fail to realize that, as expressed by Mr. Simon Winchester in Robert Bork's *Slouching Towards Gomorrah*, "...such things can only tempt those who verge on such acts to take a greater interest in them." Surely my parents never knew that a particular movie called *Go Ask Alice*, about drug use, would pique the interest of their oldest boy.

I make these points and share these statistics to illustrate how much these mediums are being consumed and how much detrimental information is out there. What then will you do about it? How much of it will you allow to be consumed and what kind of programming will you allow in your home? Will you extend a *Fair Warning* to your children about the negative effects of the media? Are you willing to take the time to seek out the healthy, value-oriented programming that is out there? Are you willing to help your kids properly judge what they view?

While growing up, none of my friends had any guidelines or specifications in their homes about what could or couldn't be watched and when. The use of the TV and various other media was a sort of entertainment free-for-all. I believe that such free-reign adds to the dulling of the senses that precedes low personal performance and poor decision-making skills. We are now witnessing this in large segments of my generation.

A severe dulling of the senses occurred in the life of Jeremy Strohmeyer, 18, of Long Beach, Calif. Strohmeyer allegedly raped and strangled 7 year-old Sherice Iverson, while vacationing in a Primm, NV. casino.

In June 1997, *People Magazine* reported, "Little in Strohmeyer's apparently ordinary, middle-class background — his mother, Winifred, is a marketing executive; his father, John, a well-to-do real estate investor — seems to account for the callousness of the murder of which he is accused." But a deeper look reveals a bit more. Jeremy had recently dropped out of athletics, and his grades dropped dramatically. He was suspected of using methamphetamines and was temporarily kicked out of his house for repetitive curfew violations. Also reported in *People*, "And there was another hint of a darker side. A friend, Andy Edling, says that earlier this year, Strohmeyer had showed him an extensive collection of pornographic photos culled from the internet. 'What struck me most was the little children,' Edling says. 'I thought it was gross, and he just laughed.'" This frightening scenario begs the questions: How much media was he allowed to access over the years? How much impact did this consumption of internet smut have on his apparent decision to commit such an act?

Eugene L. Roberts, a great teacher and athletic coach, wrote of a life-changing event that took place during his adolescence. While growing up he had drifted aimlessly with the wrong kind of friends. One night while hanging around he saw a large group entering the local tabernacle. He had nothing better to do so he wandered in. He met up with some friends, and they settled next to a group of girls who seemed to promise some amusement. They had no interest in the message that was coming from the pulpit and immediately began with their disruptive antics. Right in the midst of their disturbance, he writes, "There thundered from the pulpit the following statement:

"'You can't tell the character of an individual by the way he does his daily work. Watch him when his work is done. See where he goes. Note the companions he seeks, and the things he does when he may do as he pleases. Then you can tell his true character.'

"I looked up toward the rostrum," Roberts continues, "because I was struck with this powerful statement.

"The speaker went on to make this comparison. He said, 'Let us take the eagle, for example. This bird works as hard and as efficiently as any other animal or bird in doing its daily work. It provides for itself and its young by the sweat of its brow, so to speak; but when its daily work is over and the eagle has time to do as it pleases, note how it spends its recreational moments. It flies in the highest realms of heaven, spreads its wings and bathes in the upper air, for it loves the pure, clean atmosphere and the lofty heights.

"'On the other hand, let us consider the hog. This animal grunts and grubs and provides for its young just as well as the eagle; but when its working hours are over and it has some recreational moments, observe where it goes and what it does. The hog will seek out the muddiest hole in the pasture and will roll and soak itself in filth, for this is the thing it loves. People can be either eagles or hogs in their leisure time.'

"Now when I heard this short speech," writes Gene Roberts, "I was dumfounded. I turned to my companions abashed for I was ashamed to be caught listening. What was my surprise to find everyone of the gang with his attention fixed upon the speaker and his eyes containing a far-away expression.

"We went out of the tabernacle that evening rather quiet and we separated from each other unusually early. I thought of that speech all the way home. I classified myself immediately as of the hog family. I thought of that speech for years. That night there was implanted within me the faintest beginnings of ambition to lift myself out of the hog group and to rise to that of the eagle.

"There was instilled in me that evening, the urge to help fill up the mud holes in the social pasture so that those people with hog tendencies would find it difficult to wallow in recreational filth. As a result of constant thinking about that speech, I was stirred to devote my whole life and profession toward developing wholesome recreational activities for the young people, so that it would be natural and easy for them to indulge in the eagle-type of leisure." (Raymond Brimhall Holbrook & Esther Hamilton Holbrook, *The Tall Pine Tree*, n.p., 1988, pp.111-113)

There are two points working here. The first is that this man was changed forever because of one good message. He was in the right place at the right time and heard a message that stirred him to wake up and change. If the average time spent viewing unproductive media can be cut in half, or even by one quarter, a more productive activity or message can be put in its place, which might actually change a life forever. There will be much less opportunity for a productive mind to be wasted.

The second point is one of overall character. What kind of children do you want to raise? Will you allow them to wallow in the mire as the dirty, old hog, or will you encourage them and inspire them to maximize their potential and soar as the eagle? Kids deserve to learn that the way in which they spend their private time has much to do with who they become and what they represent. There are numerous books, activities, and programs to encourage your child to "love the pure clean atmosphere of the lofty heights." You simply need to take the time to identify those activities most appropriate for your children and encourage their participation.

This is by no means a commentary against all forms of leisure via media. I have my favorite sports stars and consume my weekly sports fix. I have my favorite music, which some may find rather, well, noisy! And I have a few TV shows I enjoy watching, which probably do me no good whatsoever. But all of these things are enjoyed in strict moderation two to four hours each week between 8:00 and 10:00 PM is plenty for us, and because of the poor quality of programming today, it's all we will personally condone. We have altogether boycotted R-rated movies.

Our children will not be sheltered from all modern media, they shouldn't be. But what they watch, and how often they watch it will be strictly monitored. I don't want my children to have an incorrect perspective of the players in the media as William Bennett has phrased it to, "confuse fame with importance." Children will benefit in a variety of ways if parents actively seek out and present their children with many true heroes to look up to.

The wise Sir Gallahad once proclaimed, "My strength is as the strength of ten because my heart is pure!" His heart was pure because his mind was free from the world's impurities, he used his leisure time in the highest heights and became a man of great strength and influence.

I recently read a comic strip by John McPherson depicting two mechanics talking with a customer. The first mechanic said to the patron, "Wade here thinks it's your distributor; but I happen to think it's your carburetor. So we made a compromise and changed your water pump."

There is no question that all of us, and especially our children, are heavily persuaded by every form of modern media. Don't compromise your child's future by neglecting to make the needed *repairs.*

Enjoy what is worthwhile and enlightening in the media. Learn from that which is educational. Follow your favorite teams, rent good movies, and buy uplifting CDs. But rise above the smut which dominates the media. Shun the baseless talk shows, soap operas, and game shows. Keep pornography away form your home, especially from your children. Find out what your kids are listening to, what they are watching, and what they are reading and be sure you approve. Limit the time they have to use the media as a leisure activity. One day they will thank you for your concern and direction.

CHAPTER 9:

The Party Scene

Even now, when the dangers of drug abuse are well understood, many educated people still discuss the drug problem in almost every way except the right way...They rarely speak plainly- drug use is wrong because it is immoral and it is immoral because it enslaves the mind and destroys the soul.

- James Q. Wilson, UCLA

One summer afternoon I watched my friend Kevin singe his eyelashes and eyebrows completely off. We were in the fourth grade then and were out at his backyard table where he was making a *joint*, basil leaves and oregano rolled in typing paper. Lighting the end of his stogie, Kevin confidently inhaled. Once lit, it acted as a bellows, immediately engulfing the entire concoction, burning off whatever follicles were in range while sending a harsh stream of smoke and ash down his windpipe. All of this was followed by a fit of coughing and hacking.

Innocent curiosity? Maybe. For me, it was. I felt guilty being there since I knew I was flirting with something I shouldn't. Kevin on the other hand, despite his near death experience, went on to become well-known throughout the high schools as the guy who could always "get you some weed." This was due in part because he had no sense of conscience about what he did. After all, he was only doing what his older brothers did and what was allowed by uninterested parents.

My oldest brother, Greg, recalls his first curiosities about drugs. It was one night when he was about thirteen years old. He watched a very popular movie called *Go Ask Alice*. The movie is a portrayal of a young girl who has serious drug problems. It depicts the specifics of drug use, its highs and lows. The story of this young girl piqued his curiosity. His continual reflections on this movie finally overcame his knowledge of right and wrong, and within the year he found his first opportunity to experiment with drugs. For Greg, it was the beginning of a 15 year battle, which would take him to the depths of the horrible world of drug abuse.

Greg's experience was not unlike that of most people who end up with drug problems. Whether it's alcohol, nicotine, or harder drugs, most people are exposed to them in one form or another at a very early age. There is a dangerous mind set among today's parents who tend to think, "Oh, not my child. He's too young. He runs around with good kids."

One well-intentioned mother I knew had a very carefree attitude about her good little kids. She loved them so much that she was sure they could do no wrong. Why, they dressed very nicely and had a great group of little friends. She assumed that her two boys and two girls were too young to be getting into any real trouble. She trusted them so much that they were allowed to come and go as they pleased making it possible for her to work late into the evenings. Her 13 year-old daughter seemed to be a great baby-sitter.

The result? They were given the shelter and physical supervision necessary to sustain life, and everyone got along pretty well and enjoyed a lot of good times, but that was all. They were left to learn about life without any counsel, warning, or real discipline whatsoever.

In junior high that home became known as the *hang-out* house. Every day before mom came home, the kids would gather to smoke marijuana, drink hard liquor, and entertain boyfriends and girlfriends in empty rooms. This trend continued in high school, and mom continued to arrive home just after the mess was straightened up as the last few kids were leaving. The kids who were leaving would flash an innocent smile and say good night just when she came home from work.

Today all of her children (now young adults), are wallowing in drug problems and are struggling to realize a successful future. Two of them never even graduated from high school. To this day I wonder if this mother has any idea what was going on while she was, "...certain her kids were good kids."

And that's just it. They were great kids, each of them. But the greatest of kids, left unattended and unaccountable for anything, will squander their potential with the temporary pleasures surrounding them. And I assure you that your kids will be surrounded by many dangerous, temporary pleasures much earlier than you might think.

As I mentioned in the introduction, I was first offered marijuana when I was in the sixth grade. There were kids in my junior high school who were coming to class drunk. Usually, they stole alcohol from their parents' liquor cabinet before leaving the house. As a freshman, I had numerous acquaintances and a few good friends who became heavy users of cocaine and LSD.

In a recent survey of 12 to17 year-olds, over half said heroine and cocaine are extremely accessible. The University of Michigan's Institute for Social Research reports that daily marijuana use among eighth graders has more than quadrupled since 1992.

In a recent recording of *The Hanukkah Song* by Adam Sandler, the crowd of students in Santa Barbara, CA cheered most enthusiastically when he urged, "So smoke your mari-juani-ka, and drink your gin and tonic-ka!" Just this week I listened to the announcement of an upcoming concert on a local radio station. After the DJ announced the outdoor location he commented that it was the perfect venue for, "Smoking pot late into the night!"

I have a friend who comes from a family who takes the *little* slip-ups of adolescents seriously. His family considers any flirtation with alcohol and cigarettes as a possibly large problem in embryo. They dealt with such concerns effectively and in harmony.

Now in his 20s, my friend shares this story of one of his early experiences with the *Party Scene*:

When I was about twelve years old, My mom used to drop me off on some evenings to watch a movie with friends. On one occasion, I met up with my friends as usual, and we had about an hour before our movie began.

We were all horsing around as young boys do; riding our skateboards through the plaza and just wasting time. After awhile I noticed a few of the guys huddling together near the alleyway in the back of the theater.

I went over and saw one of the younger kids taking a drag off a cigarette. All of the other boys were eagerly grabbing for the next puff. As I watched, we all moved back further until we were behind the theater. Everyone laughed and giggled because this was not just any cigarette, this was a clove cigarette!

"Here man, give it to me, give it to me!" One of them said as they all scrambled after it. "lick your lips after you take a puff, it tastes like candy!" said someone else. Another bragged, "Oh man, my head is buzzing. Give me that thing again!" And on and on they continued.

It was dark now and I started to look around to see if anyone could see us. I was making sure the coast was clear as I struggled with the thought of trying it myself. They lit another one, and I was very intrigued at this point. My heart was pounding and I remembered how often I had been counseled by my parents about what to do in such circumstances, but when it finally came my way, I went ahead and took it.

I had barely inhaled when I nervously looked out into the parking lot and saw two headlights driving directly towards us. We were all standing behind the trash bin and I peered out towards the headlights. My face was caught directly in the beam of light as smoke whirled from my mouth. My heart raced frantically as I recognized the truck. It was my big brother! How he knew where I was and what I was up to I will never know.

I was caught red handed. He honked his horn and waved me over to him. All of my little cohorts scattered like rats. Very reluctantly I walked to the truck and he simply said, "Get in the truck, I'm taking you home so you can tell mom and dad about this."

My brother dropped me off at home and I walked upstairs to tell my dad what had happened. I was disheartened to find him lifting weights. He was wearing a white T-shirt and gray sweats. He strangely looked as if he were a hardened criminal who was pumping iron in the yard. I finally found the courage to tell him why I was home so early and he took me downstairs to have, "a little chat with your mother."

The three of us sat together on the couch. I sat between them and my mom put her arm around me as we talked about what went on. They asked me why I had gone against what they had taught me over the years. they reminded me of our personal beliefs against such things and reminded me why such decisions are so significant. My mom made it very clear that this was very *disappointing news to them. My heart was pained because I had obviously hurt my parents.*

My friend pointed out that there was no yelling involved. There was no humiliation or threats. But there was obvious disappointment, sadness, and real concern. I found it touching when he told me that after about 20 minutes of counsel, each of his parents gave him a hug and expressed how much they loved him and that they were there to help him and listen to him.

He said that at the end of the discussion he was very surprised when his dad turned to him and asked, "So, do you want to go see the rest of that movie?" "Really?" he asked. "Well, can I trust you or not?" He went back to the movies that night, and his friends learned that in his family, those kinds of things were serious. I was impressed at the ability of these parents to show an increase of love and trust after their reproof.

The result over the years was that he made it. He did falter now and again, but his deeply instilled belief that certain activities could eventually ruin his life won out. He was never told that it was not *fun* to be involved, but that the *fun* was simply not worth the risks. He understood that the *fun* was only temporary. He told me that he, "could never so much as consider drug and alcohol use without it being a very serious moral dilemma." He looks forward to teaching his children the important values he was taught.

Interestingly, the other boys involved that night went in the opposite direction. They had no real reason to stay away from the *Party Scene* and went along with it. There was no such thing as a *moral dilemma* when faced with drugs and alcohol. One boy began high school as a star football player. By his sophomore year he quit the team, and then dropped out of school altogether during his junior year as a result of a serious alcohol problem.

There is an incredible lack of *moral dilemma* within American youth which makes it very easy for them to become involved in this *Party Scene*. With so much *fun* to be had, young people rarely see through it on their own. I am certain that personally I couldn't have seen things clearly without guidance.

The odds seem stacked against children these days. Many are able to get whatever they want so easily and at a moment's notice. There are plenty of peers, drug dealers, and even siblings who are willing to introduce children to the *Party Scene*. These people expose and introduce children to these dangerous alternatives because they can profit financially, justify their own behavior by bringing others in or they become *cool* in the eyes of these inexperienced youth.

In some cases, youth run into personal problems with alcohol and drugs simply because of what they see at home; alcohol and drugs are a normal part of life there. When, at a minimum, parents drink, smoke, or take drugs in the home, it is usually not a question of *if* that child will do likewise, but *when?*

I once had neighbors whom I happen to know were a typical *social* drinking family not unlike millions of families. They were very nice people. One day, I was shooting baskets with their 16 year-old son and out of curiosity I asked him, "Hey, do your parents mind if you drink sometimes?" "Heck yeah." he said. "Are you kidding? They would ground me if they knew I was drinking before I was 21, or at least in college."

Digging a little deeper I then asked, "Do you think you'll drink much when you do get to college or when you turn 21?" With a big grin he bragged, "Right now, I just don't get caught. But you wait and see, Chavez, when I'm outta the house, I'm gonna drink like a madman!"

While it was good that his parents didn't allow drinking

while under age, they made very little attempt to actually teach him that he would be better off if he didn't drink at all. For him, drinking was in no way discouraged, only postponed.

In the Dec.9, 1996 issue of *Time Magazine*, Mark Keiman, a UCLA professor who specializes in national drug policy reminds us that amidst all the talk of various types of drug use and increasing rates we should not ignore the powerful fact that, "...the No. 1 drug of abuse among high school kids: alcohol."

Why are so many parents willing to expose their children to such glaring risks? Sure, there are lots of people who don't seem to have a problem with smoking and drinking outside of the unavoidable physical ailments which come with using such substances. But even at a minimum, do you want your kids to be inhibited by physical ailments such as heart disease, liver disease, or emphysema? Wouldn't most parents be willing to do anything in their power to protect their children from becoming another statistic of social alcoholism or much worse? Aren't they willing to do anything, including giving up their own habits for their kids' sake?

I wish there were a statistic indicating how many people become subject to alcoholism and a variety of other substance addictions as a direct result of the influence *within* the home. I find it interesting that we spend so much time addressing peer pressure in relation to this topic, but rarely discuss the direct familial influence.

Harold Morris shares a story about a teenager who was killed in an alcohol-related car wreck. Late one evening a police officer had the unfortunate duty of delivering the tragic news of a young boy's death to his family. When the tired father opened the door the police officer said solemnly, "Sir, I regret to inform you that your son was killed this evening while behind the wheel." The man stood silent and stunned. He motioned for the officer to come inside and the officer continued, "Sir, I further regret to inform you that your son was also under the influence of alcohol. This has been categorized as a drunk driving fatality."

In a sudden outburst of rage, the man slammed his fist against a bar stool and said, "I swear if I ever find out who gave him something to drink, I'll kill em'!" His agony and frustration were obviously overwhelming.

Apparently wanting to calm his nerves, the distraught father walked behind the bar, set out a shot glass and opened the liquor cabinet. A piece of note paper fell to the floor, he picked it up and read these words:

Dad,
Went out with the guys today, and we took a fifth of vodka...
We knew you wouldn't mind! See ya later...
 - Andy

I do not suggest that doing what it really takes to protect your kids from the *Party Scene* will be easy. It is never easy, but it is always absolutely necessary.

One day while working, I overheard a bunch of young kids talking with a security guard hired to keep an eye on this particular strip mall. I looked over just as he sat down and took a cigar from his shirt pocket. As he lit it and took the first puff, the kids crowded around him in awe. I was disgusted by the way this 20-something, so-called security guard was obviously showing off for the admiring little kids.

As one would expect, a brave, obnoxious little boy said, "Hey, let me try some of that! I've had one before, let me see it. I'll show you."

The guard just chuckled a little and started to look around. He had no idea that I was watching him. "No, you better not."

he said with a puff of cigar smoke.

But the annoying little guy persisted and a few of the other little kids egged him on. "Just let him try it," one girl chided. To my amazement, this security guard finally relented and started to hand the cigar to the boy who couldn't have been more than 9 or 10 years old.

Just then, I stepped out from beside my car and shouted, "Hey, what kind of security guard do you think you are? Keep that kind of thing to yourself!" All heads snapped like slingshots in my direction. Some people were sitting around eating lunch and sipping coffee; everyone looked over. The young kids high-tailed it out of there, and this pathetic, embarrassed individual smirked and said, "Well, he did ask for it." There are far too many people willing to give your kids whatever they ask for.

Many of my generation are just now finding out some of the more serious consequences connected to certain actions. What will the next generation be taught prior to their moment of decision? Will they know why they shouldn't be involved in high risk behavior? Will they understand all of the possible repercussions of these decisions?

Somewhere I read about a clever individual who tried to escape his consequences. Upon returning home from a brief trip, he received a fine from the city which he had been visiting. The fine was the result of an apparent traffic violation. He had been cited for running a stop sign. He was infuriated because he had never been pulled over for such a thing. As he read on, his anger increased as he found that the infraction was actually recorded by a new *photographic sensory system*. When he failed to completely stop, a photograph was taken of his license plate, and the fine was promptly mailed.

Indignantly, this man conjured up a clever response. He proceeded to gather ten and twenty dollar bills which totaled the fine amount of $140. They were laid out across the table and he took a picture of the money, placed it in the return envelope, and therefore, *paid* that pesky fine! He showed them what he thought of their photo technology.

Weeks passed and the man, thinking he had *shown them*, had by now forgotten the incident. To his surprise, he received another notice from the offended city. Enclosed was a second notice of the fine. Along the bottom was a handwritten note which read: *Please pay up, or....* There was an arrow directing him to view the next page. He did so and found a full page picture of handcuffs!

Reluctantly he decided to pay the fine.

Eventually, we all must face the consequences of our actions. Give your kids a *Fair Warning* concerning this. Help them avoid the serious consequences of this *Party Scene*. Rarely does anyone move to more serious drugs without having experimented with alcohol and cigarettes first. If you really don't want to see your children become involved in marijuana, cocaine, methamphetamines, heroine, and the like; then start by teaching them to avoid alcohol and cigarettes at all costs. Set up serious rules and don't allow room for rationalization or compromise in this area. Everyone I know in my age group who now struggles with drug problems began with alcohol and cigarettes.

When, as in many cases, kids don't seem to end up going off the deep end and everything seems to be *just good fun*, they still run the risk of developing serious problems years later. They can become violent later in life, lose a job in their 40s, lose a family, or move to more serious drugs; this, after they have long since left your care. Parents who fail to teach and warn about these dangers or even encourage them through their bad example are not without some responsibility when the serious problems surface years later. Remember, while they may not all become drug addicts or drunks, many may not be able to avoid the consequences of health problems mentioned previously and a host of other consequences as well.

Seriously consider making a sacrifice for your children. Whether it be time, counseling, deeper relationships, or giving up your own temporary pleasures, isn't it worth diminishing the high risks for them? Wouldn't this add greater satisfaction to your own life as well as theirs?

I once heard a story of a builder who was hired to construct a home for a very wealthy man. This man was so wealthy in fact, that he told the builder that he planned to pay top dollar. "Spare no expense!" he said. "I refuse to accept anything but the very best."

The builder happened to be going through some difficult times financially, so he decided to skimp a little on the quality. He knew that he could make the structure *appear* as though it were top quality, while saving thousands for himself. He would accomplish this using lower quality materials beneath the surface and take less time by eliminating quality details not noticed on the exterior.

When the job was finally completed, the customer complimented the contractor on what seemed to be a job well done. The builder gave him his set of keys, and gladly the new owner paid top dollar for the new home. He wrote a check for the entire amount.

Then, without warning, the wealthy gentleman turned to the young builder and said, "Friend, I already have a beautiful home like this. So, as a gift, now I want to give this home to you. I hope you and your family will enjoy living in the finest home you were able to build."

The man's heart ached. He earned a few thousand dollars

because he skimped on the job. Now he has a beautiful home, but in his heart and shortly when he faces needed repairs, he will be reminded of what could have been.

We owe it to our children and to ourselves to decide now not to skimp when it comes to raising our families. Set up guidelines, rules, and standards, which will give your children the advantage they deserve, and you will never be left to ask, "what could have been?"

In the end, of course, kids will decide for themselves what they will do. Some may still choose the dangerous *Party Scene*, but you will take comfort knowing you did not *skimp* on your children.

This topic touches an especially sensitive cord in me. I have watched numerous friends struggle under the terrible burdens of alcohol and drug abuse. Closer to home, I watched my brother, Greg, squander many valuable years because of his decision to join the *Party Scene* while in his teens. I witnessed his progression from marijuana to the devastating effects of crack and crystal methane use. I watched my parents mourn for their son. They spent thousands of dollars for drug re-hab. Thousands of dollars, which they really did not have to spend. I watched him nearly lose his own family. After about 15 years of failure, we all wondered if he would ever make it back.

Finally in 1995, Greg did make it back. Our family considers it a miracle. Yes, he had been given *Fair Warning* years ago and chose his path anyway. But it was these same *Warnings*, which finally brought him back and which helped him to never give up trying. Had he never been given such *Warnings*, Greg would have been forever lost to the streets many years ago.

In the August 26, 1996 *Newsweek*, Wayne Wiebel, an epidemiologist at the University of Illinois at Chicago, offered an important scenario. "We are unprepared [as a nation]," he says, "especially to help the young users who are just getting hooked.

There are only two pots of money," says Wiebel. "One is for prevention, mostly through schools; and the other is treatment for casualties that have already been fully impacted in their problem. There's virtually nothing in the middle or early prevention." From where he stands, the new wave of alcohol, marijuana, and heroine use, and our reaction to it, looks horrifyingly familiar. It's going to "unfold like the crack epidemic," he says, "and we're not going to be able to do a heck of a lot about it."

Parents are the only real hope in this arena. No one has more influence with your child than you, if only you will act. Money is not the answer. And the schools are not equipped to do it for you (nor should they be expected to).

Inevitably, many will wander into the *fun* and seemingly *harmless* experiences with alcohol and drug use, which can quickly become a dark and dangerous forest. The exit from which can be very difficult to make. But you, the parent are like no other and can lead them through the unavoidable pressures to participate in the *fun* and *harmless* situations of drug and alcohol use. You may help them avoid getting lost in the forest altogether. Or, you may have the more difficult task of going into the forest and attempt to lead him/her back out as my parents finally did for our big brother.

In the classic, *Les Miserables*, Victor Hugo beautifully illustrates one such *rescue* from one of life's forests. In this instance the forest is literal and a young girl is forced to enter. In life, though, people are rarely forced. They enter willingly, not knowing the difficulties the experience can eventually unleash.

Hugo vividly describes this forest, which is used here as a metaphor for the very dark and trying times of life. The dark and trying times that people sometimes place themselves in. So dark and even terrifying that only the person experiencing it and the angels above really know. He captures the relief that comes to the sorrowing soul when the hand of a Samaritan is finally extended and received. Hopefully, you can teach your children so that they never need to experience such a burden.

I hope the following excerpt inspires every parent to do all in his/her power to keep his/her children out of the *Party Scene* which is the entryway to some of life's dangerous forests. Second, to encourage parents to go into the forest if their children decide to go there to give these children support and attempt to safely lead them out.

In this particular instance, the 8 year-old, Cosette, is forced into the forest by the Thenardiess, her abusive and uncaring foster mother. She experiences a fear and a burden, which she simply cannot bear alone. She longs to be taken from this terrible place. She is finally rescued from her horror by the man who would become her father.

I cannot emphasize enough that the ever-present *Party Scene* is a forever-beckoning gateway to such a forest. A forest from which many cannot return on his/her own. A deceptively interesting forest that thousands of kids willingly and anxiously enter. A forest so powerful and appealing that some of its travellers can never be lured out. A forest from which many of those thousands who entered might have initially fled had they been carefully led away from it by consistent, and involved parents.

> *Without being conscious of what she was experiencing, Cosette felt seized by this black enormity of nature. It was not merely terror that held her but something even more terrible. She shuddered. Words fail to express the peculiar strangeness of that shudder, which chilled her through and through.*
>
> *Then, by some sort of instinct, to get out of this singular state, which she did not understand but which terrified her, she began to count aloud, one, two, three, four, up to ten, and when she had finished, she began*

again. This restored her to a real perception of the things around her. Her hands, which were wet from drawing water, felt cold. She stood up. Her fear had returned, a natural and insurmountable fear. She had only one thought, to flee; to flee at top speed, across woods, across fields, to the houses and windows and lighted candles. Her eyes fell on the bucket there in front of her. Such was the dread the Thenardiess inspired in her. She did not dare leave without the bucket of water. She grasped the handle with both hands. She could hardly lift it.

She went a dozen steps this way, but the bucket was full, it was heavy, she had to rest it on the ground. She caught her breath an instant, then grasped the handle again, and walked on, this time a little longer. But she had to stop again. After resting a few seconds, she started on. She walked bending forward, her head down, like an old woman; the weight of the bucket strained and stiffened her tiny arms. The iron handle was numbing and freezing her little wet hands; from time to time she had to stop, and every time she stopped, the cold water that sloshed out of the bucket splashed onto her bare knees. This took place in the depth of the woods, at night, in the winter, far from all human sight; she was a child of eight. At that moment only the Eternal Father saw this sad thing.

And undoubtedly her mother, alas!

For there are things that open the eyes of the dead in their grave. Her breath came as a kind of painful gasp; sobs choked her, but she did not dare weep...

She was worn out and was not yet out of the forest. Reaching an old chestnut tree she knew, she made one last halt, longer than the others, to rest up well, then she gathered all her strength, took up her bucket again, and began walking on courageously. Meanwhile the poor little despairing thing could not help crying: "Oh my God! Oh God!"

At that moment she suddenly felt the weight of the bucket

was gone. A hand, which seemed enormous to her, had just caught the handle, and was carrying it easily. She looked up. A large dark form, straight and erect, was walking beside her in the darkness. A man who had come up behind her and whom she had not heard. This man, without saying a word, had grasped the handle of the bucket she was carrying.

There are instincts for all the crises of life.

The child was not afraid.

(Les Miserables [New York: NAL Penguin, Inc., 1987], pp. 389-390.)

CHAPTER 10:

Love and Sex

...sex is now being made into the measure of existence, and such uniquely human qualities as modesty, fidelity, abstinence, chastity, delicacy, and shame, qualities that formerly provided the constraints on sexual activity and the setting within which the erotic passion was enjoyed...are today ridiculed.

- Walter Berns, 1976

While the average income in America remains quite high compared to the rest of the world and while approximately 95% of Americans remain employed, over 50% of all marriages now end in divorce. Income levels and employment rates remain steady because we continue to produce willing workers with sufficient knowledge to sustain the system. We send our kids to college and try to teach them to work hard, making a specific effort to see our children succeed in this area.

On the other hand, divorce rates soar because we are producing more and more people who may not have learned or been taught that successful relationships require more effort than professional or career development. And thus, they do not know how to honor their vows and covenants entered into at the marriage alter.

Today, kids are left largely to themselves to figure out the complexities of love, sex, and relationships. We do relatively little to guide them toward successful marriages and parenting. A college education, a good job, and a solid income don't mean much when you're all alone. And there are very few who want to live life alone. A 1997 survey featured in the *Orange County Register* indicated that 80% of men and 88% of women want to marry and raise a family someday.

There are scores of men and women throughout the world who are highly intelligent and excel in the workplace, yet can't seem to find the same consistency and happiness in their personal lives where they yearn for it most with their spouse and children. Their career growth and success is evidence that they possess the ability to succeed at home as well. But for whatever reasons, they are not living up to that potential.

These people gained their working skills and knowledge through rigorous study and dedication. They secured steady jobs and some even climbed the corporate ladder continuing their hard work and learning additional skills becoming highly effective over the years. It is not raw talent alone that brings them the success they desire in the workplace, but talent combined with learning new skills and knowing how to apply them.

Why then, do so many of these talented people fall short of their desires in their family relationships? Why all of the divorces? Why all of the running around? Why all of the arguments? Because so many of them were never given any training, guidance, or encouragement in this area. They were left to figure it all out on their own through trial and error. And when applying that method of learning, there will be many serious errors made.

One of my friends, Sterling Jacobson, has already faced significant problems in his young love life. He fathered one child out of wedlock and does not know where the mother and the baby have gone. After another girlfriend became pregnant, he tried to assume responsibility. He moved in with her and eventually they decided to marry. My friend found it difficult to commit to any job; and only three months after the baby was born, his wife left him and moved out of state. He followed her and tried to support them but was still unsuccessful. The arguments continued, the financial situation remained dismal, and after 18 months of marriage, they divorced. He is now 23 years old.

I remember his parents very well. They were the *cool* type mentioned earlier. I met his father only a couple of times; his mother was always around. She was very fun, always laughing and seemed to really love her son. Everyone knew though that Sterling could do whatever he wanted. From his early teens, he bragged about going to the high school parties with his older sister. I specifically recall him explaining how he had sex with his girlfriend nearly every evening in his bedroom while both of his parents were home. He simply installed a lock on his door, and his parents never bothered to check on them. This happened during our sophomore year. I am not surprised to learn of his serious and untimely problems since then.

When it comes to the sensitive topics of *Love and Sex*, I firmly believe that many members of my generation were somewhat short-changed by way of discussion and discipline in this area. So many of them ended up paying a very high price for their avoidable mistakes. I say *avoidable* because so many of them could have learned to avoid premature sexual situations had they been consistently and specifically taught to do so. Some end up paying a high price for their actions. Some of these prices are high and paid over the course of a lifetime.

There is a story told about the owner of a very ill dog who finally decided to take his pet to the veterinarian. He was told to take the dog into the examination room and wait. A few minutes later, the doctor came into the room carrying a large gray cat. There was some initial cat/dog tension as the two laid eyes on each other, but soon they both settled down.

The vet asked the pet owner to step aside. His dog sheepishly stood alone on top of the steel examination table. The veterinarian then proceeded to walk very slowly around the entire table. He held the cat under his arm and the cat continued to stare intently at the bewildered, old dog. Occasionally, he would move the cat very close to the dog and sometimes even above the dog. Cautiously the animals eyeballed each other.

After completing two full rotations around the table, the vet quietly put the cat in a cage and scribbled notes on his chart. He told the owner to give the dog a certain medication and he would be fine. The vet left the room abruptly.

This rather unorthodox procedure disappointed the man somewhat. He was shocked when he was given the bill on his way out. "Three hundred and seventy-five dollars! We haven't been here fifteen minutes! What could possibly cost that much?" he complained. The assistant looked over the bill and quietly explained, "Well, sir, you paid $25 for the visit and $350 for the cat-scan."

I am afraid, in the important area of *Love and Sex*, too many children receive a similar *cat scan*, rather than the really useful examinations and diagnosis.

Nearly every one of my male friends was having sex by the ninth grade. Frequent sex. They joked, laughed, and talked about it all the time. And why not? It was fun, and no one had told them not to have sex or given any reasons why they should wait. By our senior year, I was the only one of my male friends who had not had sex. I chose not to despite a number of girlfriends and opportunities. I was taught that I would be much better off if sex was reserved for marriage and I believed it. I was taught that I would be better off because I would avoid the risks and the dulling effects of premature sexual activity, and I believed it. I was taught that I could not afford to tamper with the creation of human life, and I believed it. I was taught that at the right time and in the right place I would have many years to enjoy sex the way it was meant to be enjoyed, and I believed it. I may have missed out on some exciting moments, but I developed a respect for women, and learned volumes about self-control.

Many people I knew hopped from bed to bed like kangaroos. In doing so, they lost any appreciation for intimacy and never really learned the true meaning of love. Many of them began to take sex for granted and would become insanely jealous when their lover moved on to the next heartthrob. Someday this practice may serve to break a marriage or a family, not to mention the myriad of heartaches, risks, and difficulties which result.

One such heartache came to the family of a gifted young baseball player at my rival high school. Some of the finest colleges courted him because of his athletic ability. He signed a letter of intent and then backed out at the last moment. The reason? He could not bear to leave his girlfriend. He could not stand the thought that she might fall for someone else. Their premature sexual relationship created a trap of possessiveness and jealousy preventing either of them from moving to the next level of maturity. Two years later at home and out of school, they broke up. This young man never did develop his athletic talent or ever attend college.

Many girls I knew in school became pregnant and faced incredibly difficult choices: to have an abortion, to face the premature responsibilities of motherhood, or to give up a newborn for adoption. Each of these choices forces a young girl into a world of emotional and physical dilemmas with which they are no where near mature enough to cope. These decisions are far too serious, traumatic and life-altering to justify the cause. Lives are forever changed.

According to the National Center for Health Statistics, the rate of births to unmarried teens has increased more than 200%

since 1960. In 1995, 53% of 1000 teenage births were to unmarried teens. When teenage girls have babies, life's odds quickly stack against them. Teenagers are far less likely to receive prenatal care, and their babies are less likely to be born healthy. Many teenage mothers don't finish school. If they marry, the chances of divorce are higher than average for teenage couples.

A survey taken in 1989 and featured in *Psychology Today* revealed that only 11% of young girls indicate that love is their reason for having premarital sex. The leading reason? Peer pressure, 34%; followed by pressure from boys, 17%; *everyone is doing it*, 14%; curiosity, 14%; and sexual gratification, 5%.

Boys also cite peer pressure as the primary reason for sexual activity at 26%; followed by curiosity, 16%; *everyone is doing it*, 10%; and sexual gratification, 10%. Only 6% of males say love is the reason for having sex.

I find it ironic that only 6% of boys and 11% girls cite love as their reason for having sex, when love is one of the most significant reasons for having sex. From their own accounts, it is obvious that teens are not mature enough to grasp the correlation between love and sex. The second irony is that only 5% to 10% give *sexual gratification* as their reason for having sex. Yet Hollywood, TV and mass media portray sex before and without marriage as incredibly gratifying and glamorous (Sex outside of marriage is depicted 8-to-1 in TV and movies.) After their innocence is lost young people and adults as well find out for themselves that gratification in such situations is not all that it appears to be.

In the May 19, 1997 issue of *US News and World Report*, Jennifer Grossman, 30, of MSNBC-TV said, "This all-you-can-eat sexual buffet is leaving a lot of men and women feeling very empty. I see a pattern among all of my girlfriends," she says, "When they sleep with men, they cry. Sleeping with a man you've known for a week is such an 'almost.' It's almost what you want, but a chasm away from what you really need."

Unless told these facts early on, it may take youth many years of trial and error coupled with failure and disappointment to finally learn, if they do, that sex really is gratifying and wonderful under the right conditions. It really can be all they had ever imagined when guarded and expressed with the right person, at the right time, and for the right reason.

For so many youth there is much misunderstanding and confusion about the right person, the right time, and the right reason. Yet when looked at in full candor, I think that most parents know the answers to these questions but at times simply neglect to lay down the best law for their kids. For example: Who can argue that the parent is not the best one to teach the details of sex, sexuality, why it is wonderful, and why it has its necessary limits? Despite what the parent may have done in the past, who can deny that their child is better off postponing sexual relations until married? How much risk and emotional confusion can be avoided? Who believes a 12, 13, or 14 year-old girl should be allowed to go on one-on-one dates with 16, 17, or 18 year-old boys? Why should they? What benefits of such dating can possibly outweigh the risks for an easily flattered, naive, and eager-to-please young girl? Why should a 16, 17, or 18 year-old boy be allowed to spend every waking moment with a girlfriend? Why should either be allowed out until 1:00 AM, somewhere unsupervised or on your own couch, for that matter?

As far as I am concerned, the answers to such questions are obvious. Yet too many parents neglect to set up and enforce necessary guidelines because they think it's unreasonable, impossible or embarrassing. Well, where I grew up, no such excuses applied. This neglect must stop so that we may raise a more successful generation.

In the previously mentioned article found in *US News & World Report,* James McHugh, the Catholic bishop of Camden, N.J. points out, "Many young adults who have engaged in sex before marriage aren't so sure they want their younger brothers and sisters to live through the same experience. But they feel restrained from honestly saying what they think to the next generation, either from guilt, ineptitude, or fear that they will be rejected or ridiculed. If everybody's doing it, and everybody accepts that everybody's doing it, then the young man or woman who has a more ennobling vision of human sexuality ends up looking like the oddball."

David Whitman, who is the author of the *US News and World Report* article entitled *Pre-Marital Sex: Is It Good For Us?,* writes, "...it is hard for parents to, say, convince a 17 year-old that she should abstain from sex now but that when she turns 18 or 21 it will be OK for her to start sleeping with her boyfriends." I can assure you that such an approach just won't work. There must be a clear line of total abstinence drawn in the sand if one hopes to be really successful in helping their children avoid the pitfalls of early sexual activity. Even if it means they, and you, might be classified as *oddballs* I can tell you that I didn't care if I seemed like an *oddball* or not, I knew that I wasn't.

I have a friend who told me of a very nice girlfriend he had in high school. She could not understand why he would not have sex with her at the time. In frustration, she finally sneaked off and had sex with someone who would. They subsequently broke up and she was pregnant within a year. Of that incident he now says with a sigh, "I'm certainly glad that wasn't my doing!"

A.C. Green of the Los Angeles Lakers doesn't mind being an oddball either. At 33 years old this basketball star, now with the

Dallas Mavericks, has yet to find *Mrs. Right*. What does that mean for A.C.? This is what he said as reported by David Whitman in the same article as above, "I am still a virgin. Abstaining from extramarital sex is one of the most unpopular things a person can do, much less talk about. From a sheer numbers standpoint, it can be a lonely cause, but that doesn't mean it's not right." He continues, "I abstain as an adult for the same reasons I did as a teen, the principle doesn't change or the feeling of self-respect I get."

Each summer the Smith family would visit their favorite lake, tucked deep in a forest.

Every year as they made the short hike through the woods, they were elated to come over the final ridge and see the *funny old tree* that stood off on its own, apart from the rest of the forest. It was large and beautiful. It was peculiar though, because it seemed to twist and bend upward as if it had withstood all of the elements nature has to offer. More importantly, though, this tree indicated to the family that they were just minutes from the final descent leading to the lake.

One year, just a week away from the annual trip, a forest fire scourged the area and destroyed thousands of acres of vegetation. Disappointed, but not willing to break with family tradition, the Smiths decided to keep to their vacation plans.

While making the hike through the woods this time, the family was quite somber and in awe of the aftermath. Where beautiful, towering pines once stood, there were now blackened and charred trunks. They were saddened at the sight.

As they came over the final ridge, the father glanced back at his family with a great smile. He pointed ahead to the *funny old tree*. The tree had again stood its ground! Not a leaf had fallen from the branches; it had been protected by its unusual distance from the rest of the forest. This peculiar old tree was unable to be reached by the consuming flames, and the Smith family delighted in its survival. Its original beauty was now more significant and appreciated than ever before.

In a society laden with so many life-altering risks directly related to the abuse of sexuality, why not arm your children with the best possible defense? Help them stand apart from the crowd. Allow them to be viewed as an *oddball* if that is what it takes. Allow them to weather the storms of going against popular opinion; it will strengthen them. In the long run they will develop great personal strength, and they will find greater satisfaction and security in their sex lives than most people hope to have.

If you know what is best for them, don't they deserve a *Fair Warning* concerning this? If they choose to go against your instruction, so be it. You will know that you did everything in your power to lead them along safely. And one day they will come to appreciate what you have done for them, even if they fight you tooth and nail along the way.

This point reminds me of a story included in William Bennett's, The Book of Virtues, entitled, The King and His Hawk. This is a story told of the great and much feared warrior, Genghis Khan. One evening, while returning from a day of hunting with his friends, he decided to take a longer route home:

> *On the king's wrist sat his favorite hawk, for in those days hawks were trained to hunt. At a word from their masters they would fly high up into the air and look around for prey. If they chanced to see a deer or a rabbit, they would swoop down upon it as swift as any arrow.*
>
> *Toward evening they started for home. The king had often ridden through the woods, and he knew all of the paths. So while the rest of the party took the nearest way, he went by a*

longer road through a valley between two mountains.

The day had been warm, and the king was very thirsty. His pet hawk had left his wrist and flown away. It would be sure to find its way home.

The king rode slowly along. He had once seen a spring of clear water near this pathway. If he could only find it now! But the hot days of summer had dried up all the mountain brooks.

At last, to his joy, he saw some water trickling down over the edge of a rock. He knew that there was a spring farther up. In the wet season, a swift stream of water always poured down here; but now it came only one drop at a time.

The king leapt from his horse. He took a little silver cup from his hunting bag. He held it so as to catch the slowly falling drops. It took a long time to fill the cup; and the king was so thirsty that he could hardly wait. At last it was nearly full. He put the cup to his lips and was about to drink.

All at once there was a whirring sound in the air, and the cup was knocked from his hands. The water was spilled upon the ground.

The king looked up to see who had done this thing. It was his pet hawk.

The hawk flew back and forth a few times, and then alighted among the rocks by the spring.

The king picked up the cup, and again held it to catch the trickling drops.

This time he did not wait so long. When the cup was half full, he lifted it towards his mouth; but before it had touched his lips, the hawk swooped down again, and knocked it from his hands.

And now the king began to grow angry. He tried again, and for the third time the hawk kept him from drinking.

The king was now very angry indeed.

"How could you dare to act so?" he cried. "If I had you in

my hands, I would wring your neck!'
Then he filled the cup again. but before he tried to drink, he
drew his sword.

"Now, Sir Hawk," he said, "this is the last time."

He had hardly spoken before the hawk swooped down and
knocked the cup from his hand. But the king was looking for this.
With a quick sweep of the sword he struck the bird as it passed.

The next moment the poor hawk lay bleeding and dying at
its master's feet.

"That is what you get for your pains," said Genghis Khan.

But when he looked for his cup, he found it had fallen
between two rocks where he could not reach it.

"At any rate, I will have a drink from that spring," he said
to himself.

With that he began to climb the steep bank to the place
from which the water trickled. It was hard work, and the higher
he climbed, the thirstier he became.

At last he reached the place. There indeed was a pool of
water; but what was that lying in the pool and almost filling it?
It was a huge, dead snake of the most poisonous kind.

The king stopped. He forgot his thirst, he thought only of
the poor dead bird lying on the ground below him.

"The hawk saved my life!" he cried, "and how did I repay
him? He was my best friend, and I have killed him."
(The King and His Hawk as retold in The Book of Virtues [Simon & Schuster,
New York, 1993], pp. 37-39.)

Although this story ends in tragedy, the verbal *sword
swipes* of rebelliousness and disobedience from child to parent
can easily wound the souls and break the hearts of parents. I
will be forever grateful to my parents who continually knocked
the *cup of danger* from my hands. I did not see the entire pic-

ture initially, and my brothers and I swiped at them with our *swords* from time to time. In the end, though, each one of us agrees that every rule they attempted to enforce on our behalf in this sensitive area of sexuality, was for our lifelong good.

Children simply are not born able to tell the difference between love and sex. Left unexplained and without rules, great dangers lie in wait for them. I hope that together we can reverse the sentiment held by many and expressed by Neal A. Maxwell when he points out, "Many regard family erosion as regrettable, but not reversible." He further states, "Many who are worried about the spillings of social consequences are busy placing sandbags down stream, while this flooding will yet leave a terrible aftermath in our family gardens."

I believe that the social problems generated by the misuse and lack of regard for love and sex can be reversed. It will not be accomplished by handing out millions of condoms. It will not happen by teaching third graders about every form of sexual behavior under the sun.

It takes one generation of consistent and unwavering parenting. Take special care of your own family garden by building a strong foundation and secure fences, and let others work in vain with temporary *sandbag* solutions. My generation has endured enough of that!

Parents do not need to tell children that sex is *bad* or *naughty* or *just for grown-ups*. Such talk only piques interest. Rather, tell them that it is wonderful. Tell them that it is beautiful and gratifying. Tell them that they will have many, many years to enjoy it. But tell them that it is so important that life is created by it, and spouses are brought closer because of it. Tell them that it is best expressed within the bounds of marital covenants and that it should be expressed where virtually every risk is eliminated.

Tell them that it is well worth the wait!

CHAPTER 11:

Live Your Religion

Whatever may be conceded to the influence of refined education on minds of peculiar structure, reason and experience both forbid us to expect that national morality can prevail in exclusion of religious principle.

-*George Washington, 1796*

Two executives sat and discussed a variety of topics one evening over cocktails. Finally, their discussion swerved into the topic of religion. They began to cordially debate different philosophies.

In frustration one of the men decided to challenge his friend's merits in this area and taunted, "Joe, don't you try and tell *me* about religion!" With confidence he continued, "Why, I've got a crisp one hundred dollar bill that says you can't even quote the Ten Commandments."

"Ha!" Joe responded, "You can kiss that money good-bye!" Totally assured, Joe took a deep breath, gathered his thoughts and began, "Our Father, Who art in Heaven, hallowed be thy name. Thy Kingdom come, thy will be done; on earth as it is in Heaven. Give us this...." He continued quoting *The Lord's Prayer* verbatim.

The friend who had thrown out the challenge just smiled and shook his head. Then, he handed him the money and said dejectedly, "I'm shocked Joe. I just didn't think you could do it."

Neither man knew the topic, yet both of them thought they did. There are many people who talk the talk when it comes to religion. When it comes to doctrinal knowledge and daily living, though, very few actually walk the walk. In some cases they wouldn't even know where to walk if they wanted to. In his book Slouching Towards Gomorrah, Robert Bork comments, "It is increasingly clear that very few people who claim religion could truthfully say that it informs their attitudes and significantly affects their behavior." Religion is much more than a mere professing of belief. Religion is a way of life. It is a set of spiritual core guidelines. It is a contractual agreement one willingly makes with God. It requires sacrifice. It is a standard of living. It is a process of purification or, as it were, "...a refiner's fire and a fuller's soap." (Malachi 3:2)

Recently on the Dr. Laura Schlessinger Show, a caller complained, "My wife is under the impression that I am not a Christian; but I am!" Dr. Laura went on to explain to him that if his wife had such an impression, she was probably right.

Why such a response? Because religion is evident in daily living. It is inherent and becomes apparent in ones day to day demeanor. Spend a few days with a devoted Jew, Hindu, Muslim, or Christian, and they will not need to tell you they are religious. You will know they are. You will find out through their speech, actions, and practices. It will naturally surface.

Just this week I gave a speech in Hollywood. My message centered on the Fair Warnings outlined in this book. Because of time constraints, I was unable to address the topic Live Your Religion.

After my talk, two people came up and asked me if I belonged to a certain Christian sect. I answered that I did, and they said, "We thought so. We could just tell."

I never so much as uttered the word religion in my talk. I never made any reference to my religious affiliation, yet some of them, (who, as it turns out, were not members of my particular faith) surmised my affiliation within 30 minutes. It really is internal and a significantly visible dimension of those who live their religion.

This chapter is designed to encourage people to review and reconsider their religious beliefs and their adherence to those beliefs. The honest religions of the world exist for the sole purpose of making people and nations better. Who among us cannot benefit from such assistance?

Religions are designed to provide a place of regular worship in which one reaffirms their belief in a higher power, renews sacred covenants, gains knowledge, and develops spirituality. Religions provide a core set of principles to which one may wholeheartedly devote him/herself.

Religion is the cement, really, which holds a person together spiritually and organizationally, and solidifies and validates one's resolve to live according to established rules and guidelines. Religious practice provides many valuable symbols that constantly remind us of our spiritual commitments. It makes us accountable and responsible for everything we do. Thus, we are motivated to do everything a little bit better. Without a religious foundation, finding the consistency and commitment necessary to effectively instill the previously outlined *Fair Warnings* will be an added challenge.

Today, there are millions of Jews, Buddhists, Catholics, Protestants, and other members of the many sects of all religions. Among those, many may profess but do not practice their faith. The National Council of Churches reported in 1990 that while there are 148.1 million individuals who claim religious affiliation, only 28.1 million of them actually attend a place of worship on a regular basis or consider themselves *practicing*.

It is disappointing that so few people attend church when you consider how many Americans claim to have religious beliefs. A *TIMES/CNN* poll administered by Yankelovich

Partners, Inc. and published in 1997 reported these results when adult Americans were asked:

Do you believe in the existence of heaven, where people live forever with God after they die?

    81%..........Yes

    13%..........No

Do you believe in hell, where people are punished after they die?

    63%..........Yes

    30%..........No

Do people get into heaven based mostly on the good things they do or on their faith in God or both?

    Good things they do..........6%

    Faith in God..........34%

    Both..........57%

Do you think of heaven as something that is up there?

    67%..........Yes

    29%..........No

Immediately after death, which of the following do you think will happen to you?

    Go directly to heaven..........61%

    Go to purgatory..........15%

    Go to hell..........1%

    Be reincarnated..........5%

    End of existence..........4%

Is heaven a perfect version of the life we know on earth, or is it totally different?

    Perfect version..........11%

    Totally different..........85%

Do you believe you will meet friends and family members in heaven when you die?

    88%..........Yes

    5%............No

By outlining a few of the things that religion is not, I think we will find out why there are so many believers who are not true followers:

1 .... Religion is not convenient.
2 .... Religion does not conform socially.
3 .... Religion takes time.
4. .... Religion takes money.
5 .... Religion requires sacrifice.
6 .... Religion is controversial.
7 .... Religion puts the blame on you.
8 .... Religion has strict rules.
9 .... Religion is a daily effort.
10 ...... Religion requires faith.

In short, religion comes with a price fewer and fewer people are willing to pay. People have a tendency to focus on what is *not allowed* or *having someone tell me how to live* rather than focusing on the depth and character they gain by learning to go without and by taking counsel. This is the reality, despite the fact that statistics further show just some of the benefits of religious adherence.

In September, 1996, *US News and World Report* indicated that the divorce rate for regular churchgoers is 18%; for those who attend services less than once a year, 34 %. Frequent churchgoers are about 50% less likely to report psychological problems and 71% are less likely to be alcoholics. It is also reported that the two most reliable predictors of teenage drug avoidance were optimism and regular church attendance.

Religion also teaches people about the tremendous benefits of service as it provides opportunities to serve and be served. One such incident occurred in the lives of our good friends, Jim and Suzy Carter.

While attending law school and raising two young children, their youngest, Michael, was diagnosed with cancer. Aside from the obvious difficulties of such news, as Jim puts it, at the time they didn't have, "two nickels to rub together, and dessert consisted of smelling the inside of empty soup cans!"

This was a moment in life when one wonders how they can possibly make it. Concerned for their little one and uncertain of his fate, while bound by the demands of school and work, this young family faced a most difficult crisis.

At the time, Jim and Suzy belonged to a young church congregation of college students. These students shared the same financial status as the Carter's, as most young students do. But they were determined to help in some way. The group decided to put together a *fund* in an attempt to help offset the staggering medical costs faced by this family. Everyone in the congregation donated whatever funds they could spare.

The students finally presented the *fund* to the Carter's. Jim and Suzy opened the meager envelope and carefully counted out $191. This was all the money these people had to give. Yet they gave.

Jim and Suzy count this experience as one of the greatest acts of service their family ever received. They were touched deeply by this singular, humble act. Because of this experience, today Jim, Suzy and their family are now reminded of what they must do whenever the opportunity to serve comes their way. Michael, subsequently healed of his cancer, will one day teach his children about the $191 gift.

My personal experience with religious activity has brought me numerous positive results. It has acted as the cement, the fundamental ingredient to hold together all of the *Fair Warnings* that I am sharing with you, which my parents taught to me. It enhances my confidence and my optimism in all that I do. It helps me, amidst my ambitions, to remain focused on the things that matter most.

Religion brings a rare understanding and patience to our marriage. It helps Shana and me raise our girls more effectively and with clear guidelines. It helps me to avoid self-centeredness allowing me to keep my priorities in order. It gives Shana and me continuous opportunities to teach our children by example. True religious principles, when integrated and exercised, help average people steadily improve in all that they do.

I have virtually no talent to play basketball. I'm only 5'9", and I can't dribble to save my life. However, allow me to double-dribble, travel, charge, reach, and hack; then I'll put up a decent challenge.

At a recent family gathering, I played outside myself. I was on fire! Not to mention that I was playing against my nephews who happen to be far more athletic and physically gifted than I.

I was rebounding, driving the lane, spinning, hitting shots from everywhere, and blocking, yes, *blocking* shots. It felt incredible! I hesitate to tell you, for fear of disbelief, but for the first time in my life I was dunking as well! My wife and our oldest daughter witnessed the entire event.

I should add that my nephews are 8, 10, and 11 years old, respectively, but I assure you that they are quite competitive! And yes, the rim had been lowered to 8', but it felt like the standard to me!

Oh, the beauty of the imagination! And oh, how nice it would be if we could lower the rim of life from time to time! But we can't. There are no shortcuts in life and there is only one way to reap the rewards you seek, by paying the price. And for every worthy goal each of us seeks, whether it be weight loss, an educational degree, a promotion, a better relationship, breaking a habit, or raising great kids; we reap the rewards only after we pay the price.

To receive the unique benefits of your religion; the price is to live according to it. I will never forget a clever but very true saying I heard from the pulpit years ago: "Going to church makes you no more of a Christian than sleeping in the garage makes you a Chevrolet!"

So what church do you belong to? Do you know and understand what your church teaches? Do you attend weekly? Do you study the doctrine? Do you believe what it teaches? Do you want your children to embrace it? Does it teach principles that you feel in your heart are right and true? Does your spirit whisper that there is truth coming from the pulpit or not?

Answer these questions and evaluate your situation. If you are not sure about the teachings of your religion, or you do not have one, then set aside the time required to figure it out.

I go to church because I believe with all of my heart that the teachings are true. That belief and enthusiasm, shared by my wife, are what bring us back week after week. Seek out a religion, ask friends, visit churches, learn to pray. I am confident that everyone can find the truth and make it a fundamental part of their lives and families.

I believe that everyone, if diligent, persistent, and sincere has the ability to see through the scam operations, disingenuousness, fanaticism, and teachings contrary to reason and believability. I simply believe that if you profess to *belong* as so many do, then help yourself and your family by being true to your beliefs. Study it, live it, and don't just go through the motions. You will then become a master teacher of all that you offer your children because you possess a greater ability to teach by example. Your life will stand for the truth of what you profess, and thus you clearly show yourself as the teacher.

In her most recent book, *Enjoy the Journey!*, Lucile Johnson relates the story of a young man's appreciation for his father's ability to teach by example.

While giving a talk one Sunday at their church, the young man began, "I was fourteen years old, it was 2:00 AM, and the TV was on. A terrible storm with thunder had awakened me, and I went down to the TV room. Dad was holding my baby brother and rocking him as he watched. The room was dark except for the light from the TV. I stood in the hall looking in. Dad couldn't see me. Soon a picture flashed on the screen that was so gross I couldn't believe it! It was really bad! I waited to see what my dad would do. He walked over to the TV and turned it off.

"Dad, I've never told you this, but it really was important to me at that time in my life to see what you would do when no one was looking. I want to say thanks, Dad, thanks for doing what was right."

Lucile Johnson was there that day and added, "I watched the father's face as he sat there. He looked stunned and then buried his face in his hands. I felt I knew what was going on in his mind. Later, this father, Evan Bybee told me, 'I can recall that incident vividly. Not knowing my son was standing in the darkness watching, I received a swift and forceful prompting. It said: 'Turn it off.'" (*Enjoy the Journey!* [Covenant Communications Inc.; American Fork, 1996]pp.153-154)

This good father was spiritually in tune. He was then more able to live as he taught his children to live. This opportunity to teach through his example was far more valuable to his son than many years of the spoken word.

Someone expressed it well with these words:

The eye's a better pupil and more willing than the ear;

Fine counsel is confusing, but examples always clear;
And the best of all the preachers are the men who live their creeds.

For to see the good in action is what everybody needs.
I can soon learn how to do it if you'll let me see it done.
I can watch your hands in action, but your tongue too fast may run;

And the lectures you deliver may be very wise and true,
But I'd rather get my lesson by observing what you do.
For I may misunderstand you and the high advice you give,
But there's no misunderstanding how you act and how you live.

Looking back, I recall a handful of kids who really stood out among literally hundreds of my high school acquaintances. Not only were they fun, smart, and friendly, as many kids were; but also they had great leadership skills, were honorable, and complimentary to others. Usually they were not part of the *popular* party crowd, yet they were very sure of themselves and popular in their own right.

Nearly all of them shared something in common; they came from religious backgrounds. They did not resent religion nor were they *forced* to believe. It was a regular family function which everyone practiced and embraced. They had a spiritual family structure, and it was evident.

As was the case in my life, in the lives of the kids just mentioned, as well as in the cases of millions of others, religion was a great help to my parents. There are many teachers, Bishops, Priests, Pastors, and Rabbis who oversee various religious organizations throughout the world. These people assist parents in their objective to raise children to their fullest potential.

Who among us has not looked to another in those times when you just didn't seem to get along with your parents? How much better for your child to have a healthy relationship with a religious leader who shares your values, rather than with just another one of their misguided friends?

As a child in one of my Sunday School classes, I was given a ring with a green shield across the top of it which carried the letters CTR. They stood for, Choose the Right. Our Sunday School sang a song with the same title; and every time I looked down at that little ring, I would recall the message of the Sunday School hymn.

Choose the right, when the choice is placed before you...
Choose the right! There's safety for the soul.
Choose the right in all labors you're pursuing;
Let God and heaven be your goal.
Choose the right! Choose the right!
Let wisdom mark the way before.
In it's light, choose the right! And God will bless you evermore!
      (Hymns, 1985 [Text: Joseph L. Townsend, 1849-1942; Music: Henry A.
      Tuckett, 1852-1918])

The volunteer leaders of this Sunday school program assisted my mom and dad by providing a clever reminder of why I should *Choose the Right* when making daily decisions. This supplemental symbol was greatly appreciated by my parents. In fact, while growing up, whenever my brothers or I would go out for the evening, my parents would say good-bye to us and then call out, "Remember, CTR!"

My friends got used to the phrase and were forced to consider its meaning as well. Even up until the time that Shana and I were engaged, when we would leave for a night out together, my dad would call out to us before we left, "Hey you two, remember, CTR!" We would roll our eyes and say, "See you later, mom and dad."

As in many families, my brothers and I would occasionally

rebel against regular church attendance and test my parents ability to make it a regular part of our lives. In the end our rebellion was not successful. With time and comprehension, we no longer wanted to rebel. Now it has become the base of our entire growing family.

This year at church we had our annual Father's Day program. A 14 year-old boy named Christian, gave a short talk in tribute to his father. After relating a touching story, he summed up his message with words, which surely rang true in many peoples ears. He said, "I am thankful for my dad. Even when I don't want his direction, I am thankful that he gives it."

Our family was like most families. We had our fair share of arguments. We had the sibling fights among my brothers and me. Mom and Dad had many ups and downs. It was not easy for them to stick to their principles throughout those many years, but they did. Our faith and spirituality developed over the years through consistent religious practice. It was that spiritual development that held everything together in the most trying times. In the end, it was religion and personal spirituality that solidified everything my parents were attempting to teach us.

In my mind, there is no question that this is a *Fair Warning* that all children deserve to receive. The rapid decrease in church attendance over the years, as indicated by recent statistics, proves that many of my generation were brought up without any religion at all. For most of them, it just wasn't part of the plan. And today, many of the *Generation Xers* I know are uncertain and skeptical when it comes to religion. David Briggs, in a recent article featured in *The Salt Lake Tribune* about Generation X and religion states, "There is less denominational loyalty among Generation X. Only 31 percent of [them] report being strongly committed to their denomination..." It will be a shame if their children grow up as many of them did without the far reaching benefits of a religious family structure.

As in all important teachings, your children will make the final choice to accept or reject what they learn in the home. Some of them will reject it. Let's just not let them leave home without having had every opportunity to develop and become the best people they can. Let's not pass up the many opportunities we have as parents to become better ourselves. This inevitably occurs as we improve our own lives while attempting to extend a *Fair Warning* to our children. Express your deepest love for your children; teach them what it means to *Live Your Religion.*

section

FOUR

ENCOURAGEMENT

CHAPTER 12:

It Can Be Done

There is no chance, no destiny, no fate, that can circumvent or hinder or control the firm resolve of a determined soul.

- Ella Wheeler Wilcox

Lenore Kimbal Nitsch was known to my friend Kris as Aunt Norie. Aunt Norie was unique and an inspiration to everyone who knew of her.

In her own words she tells of her birth and says, "My wonderful adventure in life began in October, 1918. I am sure my arrival did not bring the complete joy my parents anticipated, because although my delivery was normal, I was not. Nature had cheated me in not completing her work, and as a result I came into life with a few permanent physical handicaps. I had spina bifida. The malformation was considered to be extremely critical and my life span was expected to be only two weeks. Thus commenced my sojourn on earth."

Aunt Norie's niece, Kris Pingree tells her story, "Despite her physical handicap, she had an incredible life. At the age of 21 she finally convinced the board of education to let her go to high school. By this time they were more concerned about her age than her handicap. But she got to go and finally earned her degree. She went on to marry 'her Siegfried' despite heavy, heavy criticism. She did *everything* everyone told her she could never do. First she crawled, then she walked, she read, she went to school, she married, she tended to a garden, she kayaked, she swam, she drove a car, she lived. But she did not only live, she absolutely, positively thrived.

"At 40 she decided that there was no reason she couldn't learn to kayak. After all, you use your arms, not your legs. So after a little practice and some lessons, she traveled to Canada to attempt the Bow River. She had her friends and family drop her off at one point, and they agreed to meet a few miles down river by the highway.

"Norie set off for what was to be about an hour's worth of white-water kayaking. But she came to a fork in the river and chose the wrong way. The left fork took her off course and into a series of rapids that threw her about mercilessly."

Norie recorded, "Things began to happen so fast now that I cannot recall what came first. I do not know how it was, as if with the speed of lightening, that I missed the tree and hit the whirlpool dead center. The boat was immediately sucked from beneath me. The next thing I knew I was hanging from a huge fallen tree with water dashing around and over me. How my arms got around that great tree, I do not know except the Lord must have been with me."

Kris continues, "Norie managed with just the strength of her arms to shimmy across the tree and to dry ground. She knew she couldn't stay there long but didn't know what to do because her crutches had been lost with the boat. She crawled a little ways and happened upon a board that was just and inch shorter than her crutches. With this as her crutch she began what was to become a two-day ordeal.

"Meanwhile, her friends had notified the authorities that she was missing. They were informed in no uncertain terms that the search would be for the body, because there was no way an able person, let alone a cripple, could survive *bog country*.

"*Bog country* is a term used for that Canadian wilderness, which consists of brush and undergrowth so thick it's virtually impossible to move through. It also includes dense swamp areas, which means millions of mosquitoes. Sometimes the muck in the swamp was so thick, Norie would literally get stuck in it and spend hours working herself loose. In addition to all that, temperatures at night dropped well below freezing, and it was in bear country.

"For two days she crawled through this brush, shimmied across a dozen trees to avoid the swamps, and slept under a tree praying that she wouldn't happen upon a bear. After forty-eight hours she finally was in sight of the highway. She crawled up an extremely steep embankment to the highway, sat by its side, and waited. But by then the search had been called off, and friends and family had been notified of her death. The hours passed, and finally someone drove by, and she was rescued.

"It turns out, that up until that point in history, Norie was the only person to have *ever* survived being dumped into the Bow River. And it turns out there had been many an adventurer who had tried. Every Park Ranger in the area had given her up for dead. But when they heard of her survival, *every one* of them came to meet the *cripple* who had crawled through bog country."

I would love to have met Aunt Norie too. She made it in life, and she did it despite the odds stacked heavily against her. She decided early on to excel and systematically went forward to attain that goal. Even life-threatening setbacks and obstacles were, to her, only temporary delays.

Some parents today aren't even attempting to enforce strict standards. The odds seem to be too heavily stacked against their children. I have heard people scoff at the mere thought of raising a child to abstain from premarital sex. "It's an impossible expectation!" they exclaim. I have heard people insist, "Every one *has* to party a little in life!" And many doubt that a parent can be a child's best friend, "Surely he'll do what his friends want before he'll do something for me," they say. And today, many feel that, "If I can just get her to graduate from high school, I'll be happy."

These are limiting thoughts. I happen to believe that there are millions of kids who would develop lives free from the dangers we have discussed if they were only given clear-cut rules and guidelines and then taught how and why they should adhere to them. I happen to personally know of hundreds of *Generation Xers* who lived with such guidance, accepted it, and are succeeding far beyond what is reported by the media. Some of them live just as they were shown and taught by their parent or parents. Some of them rebelled, slipped-up, or faltered along the way and many of them may continue to do so. But all have a clear path they can choose to follow and most of them are doing just that. Why? Because it makes sense. They see and have experienced the benefits. Now they can teach their children how to walk that higher road as well.

Consider how many of these people and their families will be insulated from the many unnecessary heartaches and lifelong hindrances that can and should be avoided. Someone once said, "He who cherishes a beautiful vision, a lofty ideal in his heart will one day realize it." I encourage parents to believe, regardless of their own past experiences and weaknesses that their family can rise above the negative national statistics and begin a family legacy of moral, spiritual, and personal greatness. I assure you that educational, occupational, and financial greatness will naturally follow. And I am confident that within a generation or two our entire nation will be the better for it.

In my short life, I have learned that, *in general,* we need two things to succeed in our quest for success. One is a clear vision of where we are going, and the second is a specific plan of how we will get there.

I don't know how many times I have been told or shown how to do something correctly yet tried to do it in my own, unproven way. I have had to pay the price for these mistakes many times over the years.

One such experience took place on a surfing trip to Pismo Beach nearly 10 years ago. I was excited to surf a new area, and my friends took me out the first day to a beach with steep cliffs and a very rocky coastline.

To make it out to this little reef break about 1/4 mile off shore, we had to hike down a rocky cliff. I followed their every footstep while traversing the steep terrain. I could clearly see the danger if I didn't copy their every move. They obviously knew what they were doing, and we made it to the water safely.

We stood on some rocks which were in a cove protected from the oncoming surf. They instructed me about the course we were to take, and I agreed to paddle just as they had shown me. Our designated path was to paddle in the opposite direction of the actual surf spot. First we were to go out and around a large rock, then paddle over to where the waves were breaking on the rocky reef.

My friends both jumped into the water and quickly paddled away. I was hesitant to follow them because the route they were taking was more than double the distance that seemed necessary. I could plainly see I could cut the distance in half by paddling straight towards the reef rather than out and around the big rock.

The water was smooth, and there was no visible activity out on the reef. I knew what I was doing, so I jumped on my board and paddled straight ahead. I was sure to catch a couple waves for myself before my friends got there.

I was delighted with my decision and began to chuckle to myself wondering why they didn't go this way as well. With a third of the way to go, I noticed some waves beginning to rise on the reef. The surf was about four feet that day, creating wave faces of six to eight feet in height. I was not worried though because it was a simple task to *duck dive* under the oncoming waves. As I neared the reef and prepared to *dive* under the first wave, my hand hit a sharp rock under me! Suddenly I realized that I was in less than two feet of water! Unbeknownst to me, there was an inside reef, which was much more shallow and exposed than the actual surfing area, and here I was directly over that reef! It would be impossible to duck dive under the oncoming waves!

Frantically I threw my board to the side and held on to a submerged rock. I managed to hold on as the first wave passed. As a second, larger wave approached though, it pulled the remaining water from the reef as it gained speed and strength. Now I was standing in less than a foot of water as this eight foot wall of ocean came towards me, and I was being sucked toward it! All I could do was dive straight into it just as the lip of the wave was pitching outward. I didn't make it through the wave and was sucked back *over the falls* as it is termed in the world of surfing, and was pummeled onto the now nearly exposed rock pile.

Likewise the next wave tossed me across the shallow rocks and eventually pushed me into the deeper water. I slumped over floating on my back gasping for air while trying to figure out which part of my body ached the most!

Luckily, I was wearing a wet suit, which protected me from getting severely cut up. The two holes on my knees and shoulder ruined the suit for good.

In all humility I climbed back onto my surfboard, which

now had a shattered fin, and paddled back to our starting point. Now I was happy to paddle out and around the big old rock just as we had originally planned. Heck, I was happy to be alive! I only wished I had done it the way my friends had instructed me in the first place.

Once you have set your sights on that lofty vision of what is possible for your family, once you have outlined a clear, proven course, forget the shortcuts; forget how long it may take; just commit to sticking to that course! Eventually, you will make it, and you and your family will enjoy the great rewards of having done it right!

Shana and I have identified our personal and familial visions. Our expectations of ourselves, each other, and our children. We have also created a specific plan for our family. Specific objectives of how we will accomplish our own personal goals and our goals of instilling these *Fair Warnings* and other principles we embrace in our children. We are fully aware that there will be mishaps and setbacks along the way. Sometimes we will do a great job. Sometimes we will drop the ball. But we are committed to sticking to the overall plan and remind ourselves often of the phrase, "It doesn't matter if you try and fail, but if you fail, and fail to try again!"

Nearly five years ago, Shana and I established this family *vision* or family *constitution*. We used the *mission statement* carefully outlined and explained in detail in *The Seven Habits of Highly Effective People* by Dr. Stephen R. Covey as our model. We use this *mission statement* as a family constitution, which clarifies our beliefs and gives us both structure and direction as we attempt to implement our beliefs.

Together we discuss and consider many different ways to implement the teachings and beliefs we embrace. In seeking to find the best techniques and practices that will work for our family, we talk to and learn from those parents and teachers more experienced than ourselves. We study good books, ask questions of our parents, closely watch families we admire, and seek religious and spiritual counsel. Doing these things enables us to integrate many successful techniques into our daily family life just as other successful parents have done before us.

We have found that some of the most effective and bonding techniques for familial success are not new or complicated at all. In fact, they are very simple, enjoyable, and have stood the test of time.

Allow me to share just a few of our family's regular activities, which we have committed to continue throughout our lives. The first is between Shana and me. We are attempting to understand the *Mars/Venus* factor, as taught by Dr. John Gray, on the differences between men and women. You know the old saying, "Ask a woman how she stubbed her toe, and she'll say she walked into a chair; ask a man, and he'll say someone left a chair in the middle of the room." So we developed the *take no offense rule*. This is an agreement we adhere to when one or the other of us needs to express a specific concern or complaint about the other's behavior, comments, insensitivities, etc. First, the one making the complaint must do his/her very best to avoid making any comments spitefully or irrationally and make them sincerely. The *informed* then agrees that he/she will listen carefully and not take offense to the complaint. Each of us has agreed to accept the information as constructive criticism and use it to make an honest evaluation of ourselves. We do this so that we can communicate well and so that the entire family will benefit in the end.

As a family, we are committed to such novel practices as eating together at night whenever possible. (This will be more difficult as our family matures!) And, imagine this, we offer daily prayers as a family and a blessing on every meal. Contrary to popular belief, we find it that it is quite possible to enjoy our evening meal with the TV turned off!

A poll on education administered by *Reader's Digest* in 1994 found, "Sixty percent of students who said their 'whole family sits around a table together for a meal' at least four times a week got high scores on a general education quiz which they distributed. Of students in families that ate together three times a week or less, just 42 % scored high— a huge 18-point gap." Shana and I believe this single simple act alone will serve our children in many positive ways.

We also set aside one night each week as our *family home evening*. No extra-curricular activities are scheduled this night, and we gather for an actual family lesson, if you will. No TV, no telephone calls, just family time. We play games, read books, resolve family concerns, sing songs, laugh, teach specific moral principles, study scripture, offer a special family prayer and enjoy a dessert. If it were up to Allison, this would occur every night.

Surely, as the years go by and as more children come, our schedules will become more hectic and teens might not *want* to spend an hour for a *family home evening*. But it will be a normal, expected routine, and it will be done more often than not. No different than getting them to eat their vegetables!

I can recall the difficulty my parents had with us boys when they initially tried to implement a *family home evening* program. When they first started it we were already about 8, 12, and 16 years old. We were not very cooperative, to say the least. Our first organized family nights seemed more like a *family home rumble*. Nobody followed instructions, nobody could sing a lick, and mom accidentally burnt the popcorn.

Had my parents begun years earlier, they would have

enjoyed much more success. We did hold a *family home evening* from time to time, more spontaneous than structured, but even that little bit did wonders for our overall family relationships. Today, aside from the regular holiday events, our entire family tries to meet at least a couple times a year for an extended family night. Those few short hours each year, in addition to normal family gatherings, do much to add strength to our entire family.

I am thankful my parents didn't give up when we gave them a hard time, and they might have felt that they were failing. It turns out in the end, we really were listening! We really were learning! The disappointing *family home rumbles* finally paid off, because now all of the grandchildren have a *family home evening* nearly every week. We really gave them good reason to throw in the towel altogether and surrender many teaching opportunities, but they never did.

I remember the time my dad heard some commotion in the front yard one night. He went into Greg's room which was situated near the balcony in the front of the house. He opened Greg's door and asked, "Greg, what's all that noise in the front yard?" The room was dark, and dad could not see in very well. From the darkness he heard an unfamiliar voice respond, "I think some kids are tee peeing your house, Mr. Chavez."

He ruffled his brow and thought, "Mr. Chavez?" Dad immediately flipped on the light to find our teenage neighbor Frank, in Greg's bed covering for him while he snuck out for the night.

And Brother Chris had legal action taken against him once when he turned his windshield wiper fluid nozzles outward and sprayed my crossing guard in the eye. He also had an uncanny ability to push every nerve-bending button known to parents. Chris generated more, "I've had-it-up-to-HERE!" proclamations from our mom than any of us.

I learned to push those buttons with precision as well. Like the time mom threw a glass of water in my face when I pushed her to the brink with my patented pestering. All of the mothers of the world would have cheered wildly had they witnessed that scene.

But I seem to be better known for general mischief. On one occasion, I was dragged from a movie theater and escorted home after one of my friends caused near pandemonium in a packed movie theater. He stole a foot-long strand of magnesium from science class and decided to light it in the middle of the movie. Magnesium, when ignited, burns brighter than the sun! The entire theater was illuminated as if struck by lighting! The movie-goers were not in the least bit amused, and all of us were promptly ejected.

As many have assured me, I fully expect our kids to pay us back and then some for the antics and frustrations we dealt our parents. But whatever happens, Shana and I will not shy away from the high standards we have set; we will not skimp on our children! We will never abandon the *mission* we are committed to.

As I indicated in the introduction, this book is not necessarily designed as the step-by-step program for familial success. It is rather, a reality check, parent-to-parent. It is a wake up call, if you will, for what really needs to be done to give your children the best shot at overall success. I present what is possible. I present what needs to be done, and why it makes sense to do it. I hope to motivate you to a make a pro-active decision in regard to the operation of your family.

I have outlined just a few *Fair Warnings* which nearly every parent has the ability to provide, and which every parent should extend to his/her children. For some this task will be much more difficult that for others. Some may have to make many personal changes before they can effectively enforce these guidelines for their children. Some ailing marriages need repair. Some apologies will need to be made. Some trust may need to be regained.

Whatever your individual situation may be, I am asking you to pay that price. I am asking you to do it. I am asking you to take inventory of your life and consider the state of your family or your plans for your future family. I am asking you to make this country great by making yourself great. I am asking you to allow your children the opportunity to become better than they might be. I am asking you to treat yourself to the best life possible by living and extending *Fair Warning* to yourselves and to your children.

I challenge you to commit yourself/selves to personal and familial improvement. There is not one of us who does not have room for improvement. There is not one of us who can't do and be much more.

Seek out and study the best books on personal improvement. Earnestly study scripture and other religious writings. Devour books on the family and relationships so that you might create an effective plan for implementing these *Fair Warnings* and other warnings that you might want to include. Seek advice from those you love and admire. Seek counseling or other professional help if you require it. Set an example for your neighbors and their families as well as your own. Step outside yourself and consider what kind of legacy you will leave behind for your family and for your community.

Why not attempt to live as one of my mentors, Garth Eames has lived? He is a humble potato farmer from Rupert, Idaho. In his later years, another one of my mentors, Larry Call, wrote that Garth once told him, "I have no regrets."

One day my wife and I, as each of us, will grow old. Gordon

B. Hinkley once joked, "My wife and I are finding that these golden years are laced with lead!"

Amidst the natural difficulties of old age, what a great thing it would be to look back on our lives as Garth Eames did and declare, "I have no regrets!"

Shana and I are planning to leave such a legacy of *no regrets*. Whether we succeed or fail, the point is this, if we can attempt to do it, I am confident, you can too! What I present is not unrealistic. It is not unattainable. Millions are doing it! Millions have already done it!

It has been said that, "All that is necessary for the triumph of evil is that good men do nothing." Let us not be complacent. Let us do something worthwhile. You and your children can't afford complacency, and neither can society. The risks are too great.

All that I suggest in this book *really* can be done. It can be done by each and every generation. It can be done by the generation of *Seasoned Citizen's* who are the grandparents of the world. It can be done by the *Boomers*, many of whom still have young children, teenagers, and some of whom are also new grandparents. It can be done by *Generation X* who are just beginning to enter the arena of family life. And it can be carried on by our children and our children's children!

I invite you to do this. I invite you to do this with us! If you so choose, you can make your own, "...*Good Children Great*," and each of you can become an, "...*American Hero*."

Helping Parents to Help Their Children!

BRING JEFFREY A. CHAVEZ TO YOUR NEXT PROGRAM OR CONVENTION FOR A TRULY MEMORABLE EVENT!

Call or write today and find out about Jeff's unforgettable seminars and keynote addresses.

Also

- *Find out what people are saying about Jeff's presentations.*
- *Raise funds for your school/school district by bringing Jeff to present one of his motivational programs for parents in your area.*
- *Is your corporation Pro-Family? Jeff logically explains how a quality home life makes for a more successful career and produces more effective employees.*

CONTACT US TODAY!

714-837-6742

Do you have a great thought, story, news clip, personal anecdote or practical piece of advice for parents and families? Send it to us today for possible inclusion in an upcoming FAIR WARNING collection of tips, quotes, and anecdotes for parents and the family.

Send to:

Quicksilver Press
Attn: Thoughts on Parenting
26741 Portola Pkwy
Foothill Ranch, CA 92610

Please include your name and if applicable the name of the actual author or original source for crediting purposes.